Department of Startup

Department of Startup

Why Every Fortune 500 Should Have One

Ivan Yong Wei Kit and Sam Lee

BEP BUSINESS EXPERT PRESS

Department of Startup: Why Every Fortune 500 Should Have One

First published in 2019 by
Business Expert Press, LLC
222 East 46th Street, New York, NY 10017
www.businessexpertpress.com

ISBN-13: 978-1-94897-645-9 (paperback)
ISBN-13: 978-1-94897-646-6 (e-book)

Business Expert Press Entrepreneurship and Small Business Management Collection

Collection ISSN: 1946-5653 (print)
Collection ISSN: 1946-5661 (electronic)

Cover and interior design by Exeter Premedia Services Private Ltd., Chennai, India

First edition: 2019

10 9 8 7 6 5 4 3 2 1

Printed in the United States of America.

To God be the glory and to my wife, Nancy, for believing in me.
—Ivan Yong Wei Kit

For those who took courage to overcome the world.
—Sam Lee

Abstract

The ascent of startups on the Fortune 500 ranking, displacing some of the more notable companies raised not only attention but also questions. Fundamentally, startups are built on a very different organizational culture as compared to a traditional Fortune 500. Could these cultural differences be the reason why startups are in the forefront of technology innovation, disrupting industries dominated by more established competitors and thriving in today's volatile business environment? *Department of Startup: Why Every Fortune 500 Should Have One* aims to help CEOs, Presidents, Human Resources Practitioners on how they can transform their large corporation to thrive in a fast, social media conscious and unforgiving market a la startup.

Keywords

startup; fortune 500; organizational culture; business strategy; leadership; innovation; team; training and development; organizational psychology; human resource; talent management; organizational development; learning

Contents

Contents

CHAPTER 1

To Lose US $1 Billion in 1 Day

In the early weeks of April 2017, Oscar Munoz, the CEO of United Airlines, having been awarded "Communicator of the Year" by PRWeeks a month earlier, not only saw his reputation being dragged through the mud, but also witnessed the catastrophic fall of US $1 billion in United Airlines share value, in the next trading day after a passenger-removal controversy the day before.

What Had Happened?

Physician David Dao was forcibly removed, dragged along the aisle with a bloodied mouth and his following delusional words of "I need to go home" and "Just kill me" went viral within hours, and United Airlines Club members began to cut their loyalty card and post it online.

The reason for the removal was as ludicrous as the event unfolded; to make way for four United Airlines employees and in exchange, volunteered-passengers were compensated with some US $400 in-flight vouchers which were later doubled to US $800 when there were no takers. David Dao was one of the four unlucky ones who was involuntarily selected.

After viewing the video, Munoz the United Airlines CEO proceeded with a challenging press release whereby he labeled David Dao as "belligerent" and "disruptive." He subsequently had to make three apologies in total, but it was too late as the story had gone viral. Every customer or potential customer was not only turned off by the chain of events, but many had even begun to share it amongst their networks. The disastrous aftermath was unfathomable before the days of Internet, Netizens, and startups.

United Airlines settled with David Dao within weeks on a confidential compensation which some legal analysts had guessed to be in the region of several millions of dollars, but that didn't stop a rumor from spreading like wildfire in a popular social media in China that the final figure was a whopping US $140 million. This continues to add to the negativity to the United Airlines branding in Asia and especially in China, the world's largest market at the present moment for any company.

You are right to guess that the aftermath didn't stop with the settlement. Not only was Munoz told that he would never take over as the chairman of the airline, but he was also the first CEO that had to face a Congressional hearing purely based on his leadership and communication skills or the lack of it. In Jeffrey Sonnefeld's words when he wrote about Munoz off the mark management, "Sometimes competence should matter, not just character."

Munoz had earlier inherited an airline in distress from his predecessor before the ugly incident. Confounding the dire state of the airline was also a federal corruption probe and a messy merger with Continental Airlines, and Munoz had managed to turn around the company by prioritizing labor relations which led to the award by PRWeek as U.S. Communicator of the Year. This feat he did while having had a heart transplant in 2016, at the age of 57!

In this case, Munoz may not necessarily be lacking in neither leadership nor communication skills, but the skills are mismatched to the current volatile, uncertain, complex and ambiguous (VUCA) world.

The situation is also further compounded by the virality effect of today's social media. There is always a chance any video could go viral once uploaded to the social media. In this case of United Airlines Flight 3411, the video had "gone viral" within minutes and hours of the incident but Munoz was only able to issue his first statement almost a day after. The perception was built on United Airlines and her hardworking employees without a response from the management of United Airlines, fueling the virality effect of the video. And we know by now, the first attempt at addressing the issues with words such as "re-accommodated" adds further fuel to the fire that is consuming the forest!

It's safe to say that in today's world of social media, speed is of utmost importance. However, speed alone kills. What are then the necessary components to allow one to make the right decision on speed?

System Failure

Finally, to end the crisis, Munoz admitted to a "system failure" and vowed, "to put the customer in the center of everything we do." This action may have been a little too late, however the question lies on whether if there had been a system failure across the board. Up to now, little had been mentioned about the crew of United 3411 and the 86,000-strong employees and the good works they have been doing in flying 148 million customers in 2017 alone. In one fell swoop, every one of United Airlines employees was seen as the people who had dragged or had allowed a paying passenger with a bloodied nose being hauled involuntarily off the plane.

To appease the general public, Munoz told NBC that, "We're going to teach and broaden sort out the cultural impact of respect and dignity, regardless of where you're sitting." In our opinion, the prior statement would only enhance the perception that all United Airlines crew and employees had been discriminating passengers based on the seats that they had paid.

This negative perception cannot be accurate as 148 million customers had chosen to board the 1.6 million flights that United Airlines had operated in 2017. It would be absurd for all these passengers that they had paid to suffer any form of discrimination at all.

Before making any systemic change to organizational culture, we have first to understand and define what is "system failure across the board" mentioned by Munoz; pertinent questions to ask are:

- What is the failed system that we are addressing?
- Why is the something that is "across the board"?
- What then causes the failure?
- Where is the failure to begin with and was there any lacking areas which caused the failure?

We have to address all these questions before any remedial actions. However, Munoz in his statement had provided only a glimpse of what is this system failure that he had touted.

It is clear as the blue skies in the United Airlines slogan "Fly the Friendly Skies" that there is an imperative need for an organizational cultural change for any organization to meet today's VUCA world.

New World Order

When Woodrow Wilson first coined the word "New World Order" in his call to the League of Nations to herald in a new world of peace in the aftermath of World War I, it was to unite a multi-polarized world of his time. Since then, we have ushered in several New World Order including the Cold War, the post-Cold War, the Gulf War and what would soon be seen as a New World Order built around China. At the time of writing, China surpassed the United States in economic growth. It is estimated that 35 percent of the world's growth from 2017 to 2019 would be from China compared to only 18 percent from the U.S. (World Economic Forum 2018).

What is undeniably clear is that in today's new world order or the next one that is coming along, a new industrial revolution had taken place. Widely known as the Fourth Industrial Revolution or Industry 4.0, we have marched into the era where our daily lives are increasingly infused with technologies, blurring the line of physical, digital and biology spheres at an exponential speed.

In his book "The Fourth Industrial Revolution" Professor Klaus Schwab, Founder and Executive Chairman of the World Economic Forum, describes how the First Industrial Revolution mechanized production through the power of water and steam engine, followed by the use of electricity for mass production, and the on-going Digital Revolution (Third Industrial revolution) which brought us the Internet, smartphones and digital devices.

The Fourth Industrial Revolution (Industry 4.0) sees a further fusion of technologies into the daily lives of human by increasing connectivity among humans especially, through the billions of mobile device users, giving us unlimited processing power to knowledge, information, and storage capacity at an unprecedented speed. This scenario, in Professor Klaus Schwab opinion, marks the arrival of the Fourth Revolution distinctively in "velocity, scope, and systems impact." He further added that the growth of this revolution is exponential in speed often catching many off guards to its perils and also the advantages it possesses.

United Airlines and Oscar Munoz not only shows us clearly the raw power of the Fourth but also a glimpse into the not so distant future of the challenges and potential of this new industrial revolution.

Governments have changed hands disregarding the rational and logical reasoning of many political analysts and career politicians due to it. Donald Trump, a businessman, and television personality won the 2016 elections and was sworn in as the 45th President of the United States of America with no experience whatsoever in running a government! Neither had he been elected into any positions within the fabric of government of the United States of America. Many were to argue that his personality, his checkered playboy past and his brashness, very often bringing memories of his reality TV show "You Are Fired!" in the early 2000s, lack presidential qualities.

As a businessman, Donald Trump's empire spans from property development such as the famed Trump's Towers, casino, golf courses, reality shows and to the often controversial Miss Universe Pageant. (President Trump proceeded to sell off his stakes in the pageant during the run-up to the election.) More accustomed to bulldozing his ways in business, with neither the political legacy such as the Kennedy's nor the right education or military service for a career in politics, it's of little wonder why the political elites of his time wrote him off. This political novice not only proved his critiques wrong but went on to slay many giants in his Republican party but also defeated Hillary Clinton, of the Democrat Party, who many predicted then to be the first Female President of the United States of America.

Many Americans, especially those from the coastal cities are still in disbelief that this thrice-married playboy has defeated Hillary Diane Rodham Clinton, a career politician, a former diplomat, Yale Law graduate, former First Lady of the United States and the immediate past Secretary of States of the Obama Administration. Donald Trump has not only won his opponent but with a decisive 304 electors for him versus just 227 for Hillary at the United States Electoral College.

"Make America Great Again", Donald Trump's election slogan had somehow touched and swayed America to choose him, and the virality of that slogan and the following #FakeNews would forever etch Donald Trump to the history books of our time. He had harnessed the power of the Fourth!

Succinctly, ignoring Industrial 4.0 would be like the countless horse breeders who scorned at Henry Ford's Model T. Henry Ford once famously quipped, "If I had asked people what they wanted, they would have said faster horses." One can't help but wonder if that's describing many of us who are now at the cusp of brand new world order.

In recent years, emerging technologies such as artificial intelligence, 3D printing, driverless vehicle, Internet of Things (IoT), nanotechnology, the block chain, and crypto currencies are already realities. Once considered as science fiction, UBER had test-driven driverless cars since 2017 but had an unfortunate fatal car accident in the U.S. in early 2018.

Old Money Versus New Money

Fortune Global 500 latest list in 2017 saw a combination of 500 global companies generating US $27.7 trillion in revenues and US $1.6 trillion in profits in the year before. These 500 companies employ 67 million people globally, representing 37 percent of global GDP (Fortune Global 500 2017).

Walmart continues its hegemony as the leading Fortune 500 with a revenue pushing past US $400 billion for the fourth year in a row. What is interesting to note is that three Chinese companies—State Grid, Sinopec Group, China National Petroleum—occupied the next top 3 positions. Suffice to say that this is an indication that China is now a recognizable global economic powerhouse.

The year 2017 also saw a list of 33 new companies to the global list with many of them in the technology sector such as Facebook, Alibaba, Tesla Motors, Tencent, Activision Blizzard, and Hewlett-Packard Enterprise. Some of the aforementioned such as Tesla Motors and Activision Blizzard saw themselves as first-time newcomers to the list, having cleared the US $5.1 billion bar for the 2017 list. Technology companies of these new companies also lead in both fastest revenue generation and profit growth.

The next interesting question to pose is how many of the companies in the Fortune Global 500 in 2017 were from the Second Industrial Revolution? Mark J. Perry, Professor of Economics and Finance at the University of Michigan Flint campus asked the same question and made a comparison between the list of Fortune 500 in 1955 versus 2017.

Although the comparison is limited to just U.S. Corporation (Fortune 500 is exclusively for U.S. Corporation while Fortune Global 500 is for global corporations), the findings are quite thought-provoking. In Mark Perry own words, "only 60 companies appear in both lists." What it meant was that less than 12 percent of the companies featured in 1955 remains in the list.

What then causes the previous phenomenon? Not only that the big players of its days have dropped off from the list, but some of these names are also no longer recognizable such as Pacific Vegetable Oil, Armstrong Rubber and more.

Mark Perry attributes this "constant turnover in Fortune 500" to Schumpeterian creative destruction, a constant destructive innovative force through the entry of new entrepreneurs which brings about economic growth but also destroys the hold that established companies may have.

Mark continues to argue that the churning of Fortune 500 is a positive sign that our consumer-oriented driven economy remained vibrant and we as consumers are the ultimate beneficiaries.

However, the question remains, how can any incumbent Fortune 500 or established organizations seize, ride and prepare itself for the Schumpeterian "creative gale" that is bound to happen and the cycles are getting shorter in today's VUCA world?

In an aptly titled 2016 report, "Corporate Longevity: Turbulence Ahead for Large Organizations", Innosight, a growth strategy consulting firm, forecasted that the next decade would be the most volatile in history by examining companies on the S&P 500 list of most valuable publicly traded companies on the U.S. stock exchange. Based on the turnover of 5.6 percent in 2015, Innosight forecasted that in 10 years, 50 percent of current S&P 500 would be replaced by new entrants. Besides, the average longevity trend line is also a downward slope. In its report, Innosight had offered the following explanations:

1. Economic cycles are reflecting disruptions from innovation and new technologies;
2. Active mergers and acquisitions; and
3. The "unicorn" phenomenon of active startups.

A common theme in all the aforementioned is innovation. Innovation has not only brought about new fortunes to new companies such as Facebook, which began as a startup in the dormitories of Harvard but it also explains the phenomenon of notable companies such as The New York Times dropping off the S&P 500.

Surprisingly, large corporations are not unaware that the young startups are not only disrupting the industries that they had previously dominated but are also able to build the startup into a "unicorn", usurping their rankings in Fortune 500 and S&P 500.

Innosight surveyed and received responses from 91 companies with revenue greater than US $1 billion across 20 industries on whether if their organization needs to transform their "core offerings or business model—in response to rapidly changing markets and disruption", a full 66 percent agreed or strongly agreed with the need for transformation imperative (Innosight 2016). These are captains of their industries with half of them from North America, the rest from Europe, Asia and others.

Again, reinvention and a heavy leaning toward innovation are the only means to survive the disruptive changes of our times. And innovation is precisely one of the key criteria for thriving startups!

Grow a Unicorn

Startups have been gaining a lot more attention in recent years as more and more governments are looking to mirror the success of Silicon Valley which propelled the U.S. economy. Today, even Higher Education Institutes with deep roots into traditions such as Harvard, Cambridge, Oxford, Stanford, and INSEAD advocates entrepreneurship and startups as one of their core competencies. Alumni who are startup founders, especially those who have grown them into unicorns are celebrated and raised to the pedestal as a source of inspiration to the others. Mark Zuckerberg, a famous Harvard dropout, in his speech to the graduating class of 2017 famously joked, "let's face it, you accomplished something I never could." At the very moment of that speech at the Harvard Yard, Facebook is a unicorn, and Mark's net worth stood at a staggering US $63 billion, almost twice the size of the Harvard endowment fund. Mark was also conferred an honorary Doctor of Laws degree by Harvard University on that fateful day.

The aforementioned begets an intriguing question. When and how did the startup scene come to life, that a college kid in his dormitory can grow a small idea to connect individuals to a unicorn that by 2012 had over one billion users, inspiring a movie and countless other startups their rightful place amongst the Fortune 500?

The catalyst may have hinged on these famously coined words, "It's the economy, stupid" by the then 42nd President of the United States of America, Bill Clinton, during his successful 1992 presidential election campaign. At the age of 46, President Bill Clinton became the third youngest President of the United States of America and the first from the Baby Boomer generation representing the post-war generation who had also enjoyed the largesse of a fast developing and recovering world.

Thus, it's also of no coincidence that President Bill Clinton oversaw the longest peacetime economic expansion in American history. The U.S. had strong economic growth of 4 percent annually, and the Clinton administration created a record-breaking of 22.7 million jobs during his tenure as a two full-term President, the first Democrat since Franklin D. Roosevelt to achieve that.

President Bill Clinton was also instrumental in heralding the new generation of Internet economy by signing into law the Telecommunications Act of 1996, otherwise more famously known as the Internet Act. And by the stroke of the pen, President Clinton opens up a world of possibilities on the Internet, allowing startups to thrive. We would not have our thriving startup ecosystem today if the powers-to-be then do not see the need for a whole new world of "information services" to develop on its own free will.

In short, the Clinton administration's Telecommunications Act of 1996, launched the age of modern Internet policy by "trusting market forces and technological innovation to the maximum extent. It was an act of incredible political maturity. Its authors knew something remarkable was about to happen, and that government could best serve it by stepping back and letting private investment happen" (Forbes 2014).

Unsurprisingly, the Clinton administration also launched the first official White House website www.whitehouse.gov signaling its resolve and drive to information services and the Internet. Information technology is now a buzzword, a New Economy (Free Dictionary), an Internet economy. Any doubts about the resolve of President Clinton in his beliefs that he is heralding a whole new brave world was put to rest when he issued Executive Order 13011—Federal Information Technology on July 17th, 1996, ordering all heads of federal agencies including the courts and military to make all information available on the Internet.

The Rest Was History

Two years on, the world saw the booming of "dot.com" and heralded in the "dot.com era." To put it simply, dot.com were mainly new idea companies which conduct their businesses over the Internet in the New Economy via websites that were using the top level domain ".com" Most of these companies were technology focused, but many were also trying to disrupt traditional businesses such as Pets.com, selling and delivering pet food online.

Billions of dollars were handed over to entrepreneurs to fund ideas that were riding the Internet Economy. Many of such companies were, however, without a sound business model. At the height of the "dot.com bubble" in 1999, the combined value of the top 6 tech companies were US $1.65 trillion, the equivalent of 20 percent of the United States GDP. Nasdaq was at its frenzy, and everyone was throwing money into any company which had a dot com to its name.

By March 10, 2000, NASDAQ peaked 5132.52 points (Investopedia 2011). Excessive speculations into fledgling Internet-based companies without strong fundamentals or even business model has reached the point of no return.

The "dot.com bubble" burst was imminent, and the crash was as spectacular as how it had risen. NASDAQ faltered for the next two years until 9 October 2002, losing 78 percent of its value (Investopedia 2011).

The top 10 dot.coms alone lost a combined US $2.7 billion. Their names are now forgotten but would forever etch into the financial history books:

- Webvan.com—US $800 million
- Go.com—US $790 million
- Pets.com—US $300 million
- Kozmo.com—US $280 million
- E-Toys.com—US $247 million

- Boo.com—US $100 million
- MVP.com—US $65 million
- GOVWORKS.com—US $60 million
- Flooz.com—US $50 million
- Kibu.com US $22 million
  (CNET, Nationalpayday.com, Marketing minefield,
  Wikipedia)

Although the crash was a painful experience, it provided the platform for the current startup scene today. Furthermore, the better and more innovative dot.com not only survived the crash but continued to thrive, reaching new heights; one of such companies is Amazon.

Today Jeffrey Bezos' dot.com is ranked number 8 in the Fortune 500 list with a revenue of US $178 billion, employing well over 500,000 employees globally. Amazon had also forever changed the way consumers make purchases; from trusting an online platform with credit card details to sharing and reading comments on product reviews before making an informed decision. Drawing from its know-how, Amazon is also now providing cloud computing services, Amazon Web Services to companies allowing especially startups to have an Internet presence quickly and cost-effectively.

Jeff Bezos is also now the founder of Blue Origin, a startup focused on the creation of space tourism but with an ultimate aim of moving all heavy industries into space, turning Earth into a residential area only (Business Insider 2018).

Although, startups are still known to have high failure rate with a general understanding that 99 percent of startups fail, it's without a doubt that startups are at the forefront of the Fourth Industrial Revolution pushing innovations to better human lives with technologies such as artificial intelligence, 3D printing, social media to drive the power of collectivism and more.

All these disruptive technologies are part of the reasons of today's VUCA world, and startups thrive in these environments. It's not a matter of how but when another new obscure startup will disrupt an industry, grow into a unicorn and subsequently find their rightful place amongst the Fortune 500.

The aforementioned begs the question on why startups thrive, and the Fortune 500 fear the turbulence ahead. Innosight in its Spring 2016 report surmises that's due to organizational inertia and a lack of long-term vision.

The authors of this book agree that although the Innosight finding is correct, the fundamental reason lies in the organizational culture of the company. Culturally, a startup is designed since its inception to solve an existing problem giving it a "meaning of life" and "shared values" for which the startup could build upon—the essentials DNA of startups!

In later chapters, the reader will discover and unravel the elements that forged the framework we call—the Department of Startup—that will be the bedrock for corporations steering and moving ahead in a VUCA Industrial 4.0 era and beyond.

CHAPTER 2

Meet Not Your Waterloo

On Sunday June 18, 1815 as Napoleon breakfasted off silver plates at Le Caillou, Waterloo, having just defeated the Prussians two days earlier at the Battle of Ligny and hot on the heels of the first Duke of Wellington retreating army, defeat was the furthest thing on the French Emperor's mind. General Gebhard Leberecht von Blücher Prince of Wahlstatt was the commander of the defeated Prussians. We will read more about Blücher soon after.

As the battle lines were drawn out, Napoleon's every intention was to separate Wellington from his Prussians ally, and to drive the Seventh Coalition of United Kingdom, Netherlands, Prussia, Hanover, Nassau, and Brunswick to the sea! This prelude Napoleon's triumphant return to Paris from exile from the Island of Elba, now famously known as The Hundred Days.

Napoleonès Armée du Nord comprises of veterans who were fiercely loyal and marched to sounds of guns and cannons for him, and this they did. Part of the army was also the indefatigable Imperial Guard, the creme de la creme of the Armée du Nord. In contrast, Wellington's motley army was made up of, in Wellington's own words "an infamous army, very weak and ill-equipped, and a very inexperienced Staff" (Wikipedia 2018).

The Emperor of France had every reason to be confident indeed.

From 11:50 a.m. when Napoleon ordered The Grand Battery to begin its bombardment, the emperor having rested on the confidence of his previous victory over the Prussian Army and Wellington's retreat after the Battle of Quatre Bas, he had then sent a third of his army under Marshall Grouchy to pursue the retreating Prussians. This military decision was to be one of the crucial errors to be made by Napoleon. As the battle commenced and raged on, never once Napoleon would have thought that this would be his last hurrah and also his worse defeat, even eclipsing his status as the "French star in the European continent."

Perhaps it was best said by Carl von Clausewitz, the Prussian, soldier-historian and theorist who served as a young colonel during the Battle of Waterloo, "He (Napoleon) and his supporters do not want to admit the huge mistakes, sheer recklessness, and, above all, overreaching ambition that exceeded all realistic possibilities, were the true causes (of Napoleon's defeat)."

In other words, Napoleon and his organization of the Armée du Nord had failed to see the need for a transformative change in the way they approach the business of war, culturally as a unit, having rest on tried and tested methods of the old.

Drawing from the aftermath of Waterloo, we found several patterns that emerge from Napoleon and his lieutenants which are analogous to Fortune 500 today. Let's have a look at some of the prominent ones.

Blucher Kept His Promise

Night or the Prussian must come.

—Wellington at Waterloo

It was apparent to Wellington, as he was dispatched back to London after the war, that the Prussians were the deciding factor that won the epic battle in Waterloo. When Prussians came to his aid at the 11th hour, most of Wellington's lieutenants were either killed or wounded. And he was trapped in an infantry square, a defensive position. Wellington's center was about to be smashed, and with no reserves at hand, defeat was imminent if not for Blücher, keeping his word in coming to Wellington's aid. After the battle of Ligny the Prussians had crucially retreated northwards, parallel to Wellington's line of march allowing them to continue to support Wellington throughout, instead of going east and back toward their supply line.

Napoleon had grossly underestimated the conviction of the Prussians.

It was while Napoleon was having breakfast, that Marshal Soult suggested Marshal Grouchy, whom he had sent to pursue the retreating Prussians, should be recalled to join the main force. Napoleon then had famously said, "Just because you have all been beaten by Wellington, you think he's a good general. I tell you Wellington is a bad general, the English are bad troops, and this affair is nothing more than eating breakfast."

Again, when Napoleon's brother, Jérôme Bonaparte, told him about some gossip which was overheard by a waiter between British officers at lunch at the "King of Spain" inn in Genappe that the Prussians were to march over to support Wellington, Napoleon declared that the Prussians would need at least two days to recover and would be dealt with by Grouchy.

Time and again, Napoleon had chosen to ignore the possibility of the fact that Blücher could have and would later turn up at Waterloo to engage him on his east, putting pressure on his troops and drawing precious resources from the primary battle.

Oscar Munoz, CEO of United Airlines, had on that fateful day chose to ignore the video that was going viral and to believe a version of the incident which was convenient to him, labeling David Dao, the bloodied victim as "belligerent" and "disruptive."

While Napoleon may have had time to correct his disposition, Munoz, living in today's fast-moving world of social media do not have such luxury, he had had to get it right the very first time. Both Napoleon and Munoz had dealt themselves the killer blow even before they can act upon that they might have had for their organizations.

Marshall Grouchy's Pursuit of the Retreating Prussians

After defeating the Prussians at the Battle of Ligny, Grouchy was ordered by Napoleon to pursue the Prussians, "with your swords against his back" which he followed stubbornly to the letter with a third of Napoleon's army. The Prussian was however not routed but was retreating toward Waterloo to support Wellington. This maneuver resulted in Grouchy engaging in a smaller battle with the Prussian rearguard at Wavre which he won but rendering him too far away to support Napoleon at Waterloo when the Prussians came up his right flank. Grouchy had refused to listen to his subordinate's General Gérard's advice to "march to the sounds of the guns".

For most Fortune 500, working to Standard Operating Procedures is a norm and an effective way to manage such a behemoth organization. However, in today's VUCA world, one needs to adapt with "march to the sounds of the guns." This situation is seen clearly in the case of the United Airline's fiasco. As the video of David Dao was going viral, Munoz, the CEO was still relying on carefully crafted and delayed archaic corporate communication statements. Munoz may have won a small battle for his shareholders but had lost customers and more importantly, the loyal frequent flyers.

The Attack of the Imperial Guard

Napoleon's elite Imperial Guard were committed to the battlefield late into the evening to salvage a victory when the tide had turned. About five Middle Guard battalions, the second most experienced veterans while the Old Guard formed the second line and had remained in reserves, attacked Wellington's allied troops directly. The undefeated Imperial Guard followed behind. The Old Guard was the elite of Napoleon's veterans who had served him since his earliest campaign, victorious and fiercely loyal to the Emperor. Highly trained and imposingly built and almost always above the average height of six-feet-one, the Old Guard form the crux of Napoleon's army. With their reputation preceding them, the other French soldiers called the Imperial Guard, "The Immortals" (Wikipedia). However, the Imperial Guard were severely outnumbered as they joined the battle and fought against overwhelming odds.

Why the Imperial Guard were committed to the contest so late into the battle remains unknown. Many would concur that had they been unleashed much earlier and perhaps together in support of Field Marshal Michel Ney earlier disastrous lone cavalry charge, and then Wellington could have been defeated.

Analogously, there are plenty of talents in Fortune 500 in the likeness of the Imperial Guard, especially the Old Guard, waiting to be unleashed. Managing these talents include freeing them from a top-down culture to allow them to fulfill their potential. Once they are "freed" at the right timing, not only these talents would be able to perform to the best of their abilities but also for them to "own the shared vision" with the organization.

Do allow us to illustrate with an example.

For instance, Key Performance Indexes are often cascaded down from the CEO right down to the factory floor worker whereby the CEO only sees the financial spreadsheet and the factory worker is only able to look within his workstation and not beyond it.

Often than not, the company's vision and mission statements are also lost in translation when shared from the CEO to the rest of the employees in the organization. This usual practice of making broad strategic vision statements not only cause a disconnect on how it applies to daily work but also disengagement from the company's vision. Supporting this observation is an article written by Kotter (Forbes 2013) that cited a research paper stating 70 percent of employees of companies can neither remember nor recite their company's vision. Therefore we can see that by failing to identify and to have a sense of shared vision with that of the company's would render these high-potential talents ineffective at moving the company' strategic goals at their respective work levels.

At Waterloo, when the Middle Guard beat a retreat after suffering heavy casualties from the Prussian horse-drawn artillery fire, point blank volley and a bayonet charge from the British Foot Soldiers, the Old Guard held their ground despite the panic that cut through the French lines with shouts of "La Garderecule. Sauve qui peut!" ("The Guard is retreating. Every man for himself!")

The Old Guard remained in square formation, to protect infantry from cavalry charges with the goal of not presenting the rear or sides of the soldiers to cavalry, protecting Napoleon's retreat with a great price! In Marshall Ney's own words, "yielded ground foot by foot, till, overwhelmed by numbers they were almost entirely annihilated."

We can all see that once talents are empowered to act according to ground condition and with a shared vision, in this incident to ensure Napoleon's safety, the result was remarkable. If only the United Airlines staff at the plane or the ground crew had acted like the Old Guard, not only would the disaster been avoided but also they would have won many more frequent flyers. This episode brings the all-important question on how can we achieve such empowerment and shared vision. The short answer is the introduction of the Department of Startup (DOS) into a company.

Department of Startup (DOS) and HR

What is then the DOS? In reality, the size of a startup may be big enough to be a department in a Fortune 500. Most of the time, the Department of Human Resources (HR) alone would dwarves that of a startup.

However, the DOS may not necessarily be a physical entity, but it is an organizational cultural change agent.

The DOS is, in a nutshell, a catalyst for the introduction of startup culture into the Fortune 500. The purpose is to facilitate an organizational change within the Fortune 500 to bring upon characteristics of a successful startup especially in being innovative, agile and shared vision including shared responsibility leading to empowerment of the organization's employees.

To understand the significance of DOS in the 21st century, it is imperative that we examine what drove Fortune 500 in the previous century. The entity of interest is no other than the Department of Human Resources (HR).

The 20th century saw the formation of the Department of Human Resources (HR) as the engine to propel the organization to succeed through talent management. The evolution of Human Resource Management (HRM) after that, was in many ways a response to the demands of the market of its time.

Professor Chris Mabey (Mabey 2011), traced the historical antecedents of HRM while noting several distinctive phases which contributed to our modern day HR. In his study guide, "Introduction to HRM and the origins and growth of HRM," using the United Kingdom as a point of the study, he identified, five significant evolution phases which are the following:

1. The welfarist phase—this began in the late 19th century during the Industrial Revolution when concerns of the health and safety of workers prompted legislation and formal appointment of "welfare workers."
2. The industrial efficiency phase—by the turn of the century, there was an increased interest in how working conditions affected labor efficiency or work performance. This interest was influenced by the military use of "scientific" selection techniques, psychometric tests and morale and its effect on productivity. The aftermath of the two World Wars had also necessitated the need to increase productivity due to a vast reduction number of labors at hand.
3. The personnel administration phase—with the rise of trade unions and collective bargaining, "industrial relations" came to the fore in 1930. Personnel function then became more bureaucratic, and

standardization introduced into all areas of an organization such as selection and recruitment, job training, and job design. "Human relations" began to take center stage and under the rising influence of behavioral sciences, organizational psychology and sociology.

4. The industrial relations phase—the 1950s saw the acceleration of industrial conflicts and collective bargainings, leading to the belief that "employee relations" are paramount to the success of any organizations. Communication and motivation were then the keys to reaching utopic employee relations, opening doors to research and consultancy in behavioral sciences in areas of selection and recruitment, leadership, employee motivation and more. With an increased influence in driving the organization forward, personnel practitioner took a turn toward professionalism with specialized training and the introduction of professional bodies such as the Institute of Personnel Management.

5. The HRM phase—with the onset of recessions in the 80s and the climbing unemployment, the influence of the trade unions began to ebb. Traditional personnel managers were no longer relevant and a "new specialist contribution, while simultaneously locating themselves unequivocally within the management team" (Legge 2002) was needed. In a nutshell, personnel practitioners required to reinvent themselves. Reinvention pointed toward astute management of human resources and organizational culture to create a competitive advantage for each organization.

6. Corporate strategy was the new black. While renown corporate strategist, Porter (1985), was looking into generic strategies for competitive advantage, other academicians such as Beer, Spector, et al. (1985) were arguing that the most sustainable form of corporate strategy stems from effective use of human resources.

At that time, pieces of evidence on these arguments were pressing at the doors of the Western world. Japan, as a nation with manufacturing companies such as Toyota, Mitsubishi, and Sony, were proving to the world that as a country with scarce natural resources, one can punch above its weight through ingenious human resource policy and strategy. Japanese corporate companies achieved this feat through a more collective and team approach to employee relations whereby the organization will take care of not only the employee but also his or her family well-being from education for the children to healthcare. In return, the employee would then internalized the company's value and work for the best interest of the organization, giving birth to the term "salaryman." The result was an eye-opener to the Western organization as the approach "resulted in forms of corporate culture and organizational commitment among staff which removed the need for either traditional market-based controls or the controls of a bureaucratic, rules-led corporation" (Mabey 2011).

SINGAPORE—THE LITTLE RED DOT!

Singapore often referred to as "the little red dot", has successfully proven how strategic HRM can lead to outstanding results in nation-building. For an island country with a population just shy of 2 million when it gained its independence in 1965, Singapore had no natural resources, and at 716 km,² Singapore is 1/40th the size of Hawaii. With no hinterlands to depend on, Singapore had to purchase fresh waters for consumption and sand for reclamation from the State of Johor, a neighboring state of Malaysia. The only thing Singapore had was her human resources.

Lee Kuan Yew, the Founding Father of Singapore, a firm believer of talent management and personality assessment pulled Singapore from Third World to the First in just slightly more than one generation. Singapore, once one of the poorest countries in the world has risen to one of the highest per capita GDP of approximately US $56,000 in the world by 2014. Her "most competitive economy ranking" in the same year was only behind the United States of America and Hong Kong, according to the World Bank's World Development Indicators.

Lee Kuan Yew was in office from 1959 till 1990. Under his leadership as Prime Minister, the brightest Singaporean were sent to the Ivy leagues for an education and to return as scholars serving in the administration of the country. Meritocracy was placed well above lineage, association, and inheritance. Not satisfied with growing just her talents organically, Singapore sought the "foreign talent" globally and from the South East Asian region especially that of her neighbor Malaysia. The author, like many Malaysians before him was given an engineering education at the prestigious Nanyang Technological University of Singapore, with a partial scholarship and with the Singapore government as his guarantor at the bank.

Today, Singapore is a world renown financial and trading hub, a prosperous city-state of 5 million with world's leading education institutions, healthcare, transportation and an economic powerhouse, the envy of many. And sound strategic HRM is one of the building blocks.

Classical Human Resources Management

Academicians and practitioners had made many attempts to define HRM. HRM, however, remains elusive as each definition carries certain assumptions and goals with it. Nonetheless, Chris Mabey, opined that Beaumont (1992) had managed to describe HRM at its uncomplicated form, that is, "the key message of the HRM literature is the need to establish a close, two-way relationship between business strategy or planning and Strategic Human Resources Management (SHRM) strategy or planning." In essence, the strategic deployment of human resources must first support the business leading to many HR practitioners identifying themselves as Business Partners today. And vice versa, the industry must invest in managing the human capital of the company to unleash the potential of these talents. Also, to secure the employee's commitment, loyalty and to do their very best for the company.

The emphasis on this bilateral relationship is not to be trivialized as it would eventually translate to tangible results in the company's key performance indexes such as revenue, profitability and stock price.

To further understand the model and framework of HRM, most HR practitioners and academicians identify with two schools of thoughts in what is being viewed as classical HRM, that is, that of Michigan Institute of Technology and Harvard Business School. The former focuses on strategic management via the writings of Fombrun, Tichy, and Devanna (1984) in Strategic HRM while the latter on human relations in the literature Human Resources Management; a general manager's perspective by Beer,et al. (1985).

In the Michigan school of thoughts, the implementation of the corporate strategy is the main thrust with business strategies, organizational structure and HRM designed to support it. HRM systems would include selection and recruitment, "right fit," reward, motivation, and development.

The Harvard group (Beer, et al. 1985) on the other hand, focuses on the manager who has the capacity to make right decisions that would allow the relationship between the employees and the company to flourish, leading to the desired outcome for all key stakeholders of the organization. The keyword here is the relationship or workforce relations. Thus, the focus is on HRM strategies that could bring about unity, integration, team motivation and collective values to drive the company's performances. In contrast to the best-fit approach, this model drives toward "best practices" or "an internal strategy: a strategy for how its internal resources are to be deployed, motivated and controlled… external and internal strategies must be linked." (Beer, et al. 1985).

Building on these two schools of thoughts, Mabey (2011) broadly described four broad approaches to connect strategic HRM to organizational strategy, capability, and competency. Each method has its own merits and demerits but overall allows a formulation of a framework that will work in any organization's strategic HRM.

The four (4) approaches are:

To design HRM strategies, structures and systems to fit the organizational strategy.
HRM is a tool to enhance an organization's capability to execute and achieve corporate strategy. All HR strategy, systems, design, policies and rewards must be designed based on the corporate strategy. In this case, HR practitioners would generally be known as business partners, working hand-in-hand with line managers to execute corporate strategy via strategic talent management. This classic view of HRM would either use a "best fit" or a "best practice" approach in designing HRM strategy that fits the strategy.

Organizational core competencies and capabilities dictate HRM strategy.
This approach takes a "resource-based view" of HRM whereby the first task of HRM is to look internally and then to identify, develop and deploy organization's competencies for organizational strategy development. Although this may seem to be restrictive, it's very efficient when

an organization could harness its human capital's competency for new business strategy. Areas such as skill transfer and leadership are highly appreciated in such an approach.

To focus on the organizational capability to formulate the strategy.
This approach questions the assumption that the organizational strategy is sound and that HRM strategies are then developed around it. However, what if the corporate strategy itself is flawed due to various reasons such as inept leadership, flawed market intelligence and the gap in understanding market dynamics? Here, HRM main focus is to ensure that the organization as a whole is able to formulate strategies that are relevant to the corporates desired outcome.

To focus on organizational learning and development capability.
The focus here would be for HRM to be an engine for "change management" or a "change agent" in the organization. To survive or thrive in an increasingly competitive marketplace, the organization must be able to learn, adapt and develop new capabilities. Failing to do so has seen countless companies being made redundant and subsequently filing for bankruptcy. The heart of this approach is for HRM to develop such "change capability" in the organization. Not surprisingly, learning culture would be one of the hallmarks of this strategy.

Therefore, regardless of which approach is being adopted, in the heart of HRM is the development of employees to achieve the desired outcome of a corporate strategy. And with the fundamental shift toward examining the "outcome" or "performance" in applying HRM in the 90s, the causal effect of putting people first for organizational success was irrefutable. Pfeffer and Veiga (1999), quoting an award-winning study on high work performances practices in 1996, demonstrated that "a one standard deviation improvement in human resource system was associated with an increase in shareholder wealth of US $41,000 per employee." Imagine the wealth creation for shareholders today, when an organization invests heavily into its people and HRM strategy.

Once the financial benefit of HRM was established, there was no turning back. HRM brought not only economic benefits to the Fortune 500, but it also spawned an entire industry in human resources consulting worth US $18.4 billion in 2007 alone. Human resources consultancies focus on several core practices such as:

Employee engagement
Employee compensation and benefits
Talent Mobility (Expatriation)
Actuarial and effective retirement programs
Post mergers and acquisition management programs

Henceforth, there is never a shadow of a doubt that HRM had brought about enormous success to the Fortune 500 in the last century and will continue to play a significant role in this century. The question that begs an answer will be if an effective HRM is enough for this century of rapid innovation, social media usage, the Internet penetration, Netizens influence and where information travels at the speed of virality?

The title of the Harvard Business Review issue of July–August 2015, "It's time to blow up HR and build something new." says it succinctly, that there is a need for a reinvention in HR, refocusing on people before strategy and what we, the authors believe strongly in—a new organizational culture practice via the DOS.

CHAPTER 3

The Road Less Traveled

Marriott International, the world largest hotelier with over 6,500 hotels in 127 countries with luxury brands such as JW Marriott, The Ritz-Carlton, St. Regis, W Hotel, Westin and Le Meridien, sent out a seemingly routine survey to its loyalty members in the early January of 2018. Even counting over 100 million guests as its Marriott Rewards loyal members, sending out a survey should have been a simple walk in the park for the employee tasked with that role. However, nothing could be further from the truth.

With that clicked of the button "send," the 91-year-old hotel, which began as a nine-seat A&W root beer stand to over 600,000 associates in 2017 (Marriott recognizes its employees as associates drawing upon its people first culture), went into crisis mode with the world's biggest market today, China.

Whether intentional or not, the survey had asked its members for their countries of residence, listed Tibet, Taiwan, Hong Kong, and Macau as countries. Before long, the Chinese netizens spotted the survey, and in a market of 1.386 billion people, it went viral within hours drawing in a storm of criticism. Now Marriott is being accused of supporting "separatist movement" in a sovereign country while at the drawing profits from it. The Shanghai office of China's cyberspace administration, the Internet regulator, posted online that by listing Taiwan as a country, Marriott had "seriously violated national laws and hurt the feelings of the Chinese people."

Meanwhile, President and CEO of Marriott International, Inc., Arne Sorenson was waking up half the world away to a nasty political crisis, and to "hurt the feelings of the Chinese people" was the last thing that he had wanted to do. China is an increasingly important market for him and with 240 hotels and counting, Marriott, in Sorenson's own words in an industry conference six months earlier, was "opening in excess of one [hotel] a week in China." And to top it up, China represents the single most important market outside of the U.S., bringing in an increase of 8.4 percent in revenue per available room, a key industry business metric. Comparatively, North America was able to muster a mere 1.5 percent rise while the rest of the world was clocking a 2.6 percent.

Sorenson was quick with his public apologies, totaling five in all, but that had failed to lighten the perfect storm. With words like "deeply sorry" and "reiterate our usual stand in respecting China's sovereignty and territorial integrity", the hotelier still couldn't see the light at the end of the tunnel. The virality of the social media in this case WeChat was fast and furious.

To further add to his woe, in the later part of the same week, an employee or associate had used the Marriott Twitter account to "Like" a post shared by Friends of Tibet, which campaigns for Tibet's independence. Again this was picked up by Netizens and the outcry this time led to another round of apology from Sorensen, and Marriott was ordered to take down its website and to perform a thorough revamp and correction by the Cyberspace Administration of China.

After un-liking the Tweet, Sorensen issued a stronger and targeted apology, saying that,

> We don't support anyone who subverts the sovereignty and territorial integrity of China and we do not intend in any way to encourage or incite any such people of groups. We recognize the severity of the situation and sincerely apologize.

In the aftermath, many international companies such as ZARA, Medtronic, Qantas, and Delta Air were also caught in the eye of the storm for having listed Taiwan and Macau as countries. These companies subsequently made public apologies on their websites.

Who would have thought a simple "Like" or "Share" could have brought so much controversies which could potentially affect a multi-million dollar business. A scene like the one mentioned earlier would not have happened a short 10 years ago when the Internet was at its infancy and "social media" was not a word to be found in anyone's vocabulary. In fact, Fortune 500 from the 20th century may see the aforementioned a little far-fetched if someone brought up the risk of running a social media account.

Nonetheless, the world today has changed and is imperative for Fortune 500 to make the corresponding changes to thrive in today's world of information and social media. Heraclitus of Ephesus, the Greek scholar, had said it aptly "change is the only constant."

"HELLO, WORLD!"

As of December 31st, 2017, there were 4.1 billion Internet users, a 54.4 percent penetration rate per the global population today of slightly more than 7 billion people. The penetration rate in North America and Europe stood at a staggering 95 percent and 85.2 percent, respectively. In other words, access to information online and connectivity between any individuals are as simple as a mouse click or an enter button on an app. Information now travels fast and furious, crossing borders and time zones in milliseconds. This trend will only continue to grow exponentially.

The growth rate of Internet users for the past 18 years since 2000, is at a 1,052 percent and there is no indication at all that it will slow down as more and more devices are made available to access the Internet. What started as a Personal Computer as the only hardware to access to the Internet, the past 10 to 15 years had seen mobile devices such as the smartphones, tablets to watches having ability to do so. Many more devices with the concept of Internet of Things (IoT) will be created bringing information to any individuals wherever and whenever they are.

If Alexander Graham Bell's first words of "Mr. Watson, come here, I need to see you." over his creation, the telephone, set the wave of connectivity which changed not only how individuals and companies shared information in the past century, Sir Tim Berners-Lee would be the father of modern communication for inventing the World Wide Web or better known as the Internet. What started as a simple idea of information sharing without every physicist having to use the same hardware and software at CERN, the European Organization for Nuclear Research where Sir Tim Berners-Lee worked, has transformed into a continually evolving information sharing organism which has changed not just lives but also societies and ruling powers.

The fateful innovation went live on August 6, 1991 via the World-WideWeb browser also developed by Sir Tim Berners-Lee, and the subsequent decision by CERN in 1993 to make the Internet available free of charge and completely open, had brought about tremendous change to our everyday lives.

The Web or Internet is now accessible almost any seconds of our day, providing information and connectivity at the tip of our fingertips. They are now like the breath that we take. It's constantly there although you don't see it. In major cities, you can see what's the arriving time of your next bus down to the minute via an app on your phone; you can rent a bicycle via an app on your phone and in most cities especially in China, even the beggar is accepting offerings on a mobile payment app.

While the speed of information has changed how consumers receive and perceive the information that they have received, connectivity influences how they trust and decide on the information that keeps on streaming into their devices. Having received information from a connected source via social media such as Facebook, Instagram, Twitter or LinkedIn, one would tend to trust the information more. This "trust" was something only achievable by branding in the last century whereby people trust a Fortune 500 brand. Today that is no longer the case. Big brands can bring a product to a certain level of trust but not to bring the consumer to the final lap of buying. This role has now been taken by what would be typically known as Influencers, Bloggers, YouTubers, Facebook and Amazon commenters or in general Netizens.

Without a doubt, social media is the catalyst to this new phenomenon of how consumers perceive and make their buying decisions or which political party or leader they should be voting for. The information from a trusted source, from a source that talks and thinks like you, from a source which faces the same problem as you and from a source with the same aspirations as you are highly influential.

As you read the previous paragraph, which is slightly under 1 minute, about 300 hours of video had been uploaded to YouTube, and by the end of your day, as you retire to bed, roughly 5 billion videos on YouTube have been viewed by people in all corners of the world.

Facebook has 1.15 billion mobile users daily, and the Like and Share buttons are viewed across 10 million websites per day. By the time you finish reading this sentence, five new profiles would have been created on Facebook. And currently, worldwide, there are 2.2 billion active Facebook users in a month.

Fortune 500 customers now have access to not just the advertisement or commercial branding, but information and sharing of the experiences of other trusted consumers of the products or services. And in many cases, the sharing of experience starts from unboxing the product to finally reviewing the products from a YouTuber's point of view.

A classic example would be the "unboxing or unveiling of an iPhone". Just by typing "unboxing iPhone X", YouTube returns a result of over 6 million videos with the top video having been viewed 11 million times. The YouTube is not an official video from Apple but from a YouTuber who has over 6 million subscribers, a trusted connected source. That single "Apple iPhone X Unboxing" has also generated 23,000 comments mainly questions and sharing amongst the YouTube viewers. What we are seeing here is genuine, authentic and uncorroborated information and content sharing of a product. Many potential consumers would have taken this into account before deciding if they want an iPhone or an Android phone. Trust is being built around the YouTuber and his or her followers' comments and no longer just the brand alone.

A new reality has dawned on the Marketing Department of any Fortune 500. The control that marketing has on consumers via traditional media such as television, newspaper, and magazines are fast eroding. Consumers no longer depend wholly on such marketing efforts to decide on their purchasing needs. Marketing needs to acknowledge this reality and find complementary roles within social media.

Needless to say, the senior leadership of any Fortune 500 can ill afford to ignore that a significant portion of the power of branding and marketing is now in the hands of its consumers and it is now time to adapt to this new dynamic by executing changes from within.

The Rise of the Machine

Machine learning or artificial intelligence is now seen as one of the important components in the push for the 4th Industrial Revolution. This analysis is also consistent with the prediction by Sir Tim Berners-Lee on where will the Web go in the future. He had coined the word "The Semantic Web" and described it as "A web of data that can be processed directly and indirectly by machines." The Semantic Web will see metadata becomes an integral part of the Internet experience whereby the data is designed to be read by machines and for machines to "automatically create new meaning from all the information out there." (TheNextWeb 2011).

However, artificial intelligence was not something discovered yesterday. During the early days of World War II, the Germans were winning the Battle of the Atlantic and to defeat them, the British needed to break their coded communications. German's encrypted messages were generated by Enigma, a cipher machine that had proven to be beyond the reach of the British until Alan Turing joined the Government Code and Cypher School (GC&CS) at Bletchley Park, Britain's codebreaking center.

Not only was Alan Turing able to decipher the German's coded messages, but he also went above and beyond by creating a machine, later known as the Turing machine, an electromechanical machine that could find the settings for the Enigma! Alan Turing had built a machine that's capable of learning from past messages or data, alluding to what would be known as Artificial Intelligence today. The Admiralty estimated that this new machine had shortened the war in Europe by more than two years and had saved over 14 million lives. Undoubtedly, Alan Turing is widely known as the Father of Artificial Intelligence or Machine Learning.

Artificial Intelligence or better known as AI today, has become an integral part of the technology that's being brought forward mainly by startups. AI is the new black, and the startup scene is lapping up this new technology as a foundation of their business offerings. It's not uncommon to hear about AI in Human Resources and Talent Selection, AI in Banking, AI in Healthcare, AI in Automobiles and much more. AI can be deployed in any industry whereby there is a need to process a large amount of data, decipher the pattern of these data and then to proceed to predict to a specified accuracy the outcome of a query posted to these data. And the more "training" that you provide to the machine or neural networks, the more accurate the machine becomes.

To illustrate the aforementioned, imagine if you are a HR Director looking for the best engineers who would fit into your organization's business needs. Apart from objective assessment such as personality or behavioral questionnaires, assessment centers, AI can calculate a matching ratio based on predictive analysis by analyzing data such as resumes of over a million engineers and compare them with data of engineers who had excel in your organization. This scenario is, of course, made based on several assumptions such as your organization had already identified a competency framework to measure how and what you would define as a successful engineer. The reliability or the authenticity of the data would have also been assumed to be accurate to a certain degree.

The same principle applies in the driverless car explained in the earlier chapter. Through machine learning, the vehicle equipped with the AI is taught to process and define data such as terrain, moving vehicles and at what angle to turn the wheel dependent on the angle of the curve of the corner and more.

The question is why AI is emerging only now? The reason is rather apparent. It's the accumulation of data due to the connectivity provided by the Internet, and when enough data has been gathered, it passes an arbitrary threshold and becomes "Big Data". AI thrives by interpreting Big Data. As recent as the turn of the century, no one could have neither fathomed the amount of data that could be accumulated on the Internet nor guessed that people would share data so freely on the Internet. It is estimated that between Google, Amazon, Microsoft, and Facebook, they hold at least "1,200 petabytes which is 1.2 million terabytes whereby one terabyte is 1,000 gigabytes." (Science Focus 2017).

In 2011, Martin Hilbert, professor of communications at the University of California, Davis, attempted to visualize the amount of data on the Internet then, by calculating it to the number of CD-ROMS required. His finding shows that by 2007, the world's digital information, if stored on CD-ROM, would overshoot the moon, stretching 280,707.5 miles or 451,755 kilometers, where the distance to the moon from Earth is only 238,900 miles or 384,400 kilometers. (LiveScience.com 2016).

With such a vast amount of data and the maturing technology of AI or machine learning, industries are being disrupted at an unprecedented pace. In an article titled "5 Industries A.I. will Disrupt in the Next 10 years" (Inc.com August 2017), James Paine the author, predicted that healthcare, transportation, finance, lifestyles marketing would face disruption. To quote an example on marketing, AI would be able to drive marketing efforts toward more personalization. Much in the likes of how Amazon, would be able to make recommendations based on the books that one had browsed or purchased in the past. Or in healthcare,

AI would be able to help predict the next bout of influenza, the number of patients to be expected worldwide and correspondingly the number of vaccines to be manufactured.

The potential of AI, massively outweighs the negatives that may come with it and it's a technology that is steamrolling through our century much like the steam engine which brought about the modern world in the First Industrial Revolution. Fortune 500 can ill afford to let startups leapfrog them with the help of AI.

GOOGLE IT!

When Larry Page and Sergei Brin founded Google in 1998 while they were PhD students at Stanford University, the furthest thing in their mind would be for their startup to one day made it to the Oxford English and Merriam-Webster Collegiate Dictionary as a verb. According to the entry in these dictionaries, "google" denotes the use of Google search engine to obtain information on the Internet. And search you can for the world's knowledge and the information is at a snap of your finger when you use Google search.

As the Internet began to grow, more and more web pages and data was created on it, rendering search for information to be rather tedious. The only way then was for someone to send you their specific URL or website address if you want to read their web content. Plus the downside is that you won't be able to see what else is out there in the vast Internet or who else is creating content and data that might be of interest to you. Search engines were and still are the solution to the previous problem.

The way the search engine works is to allow anyone to make a query with just keywords and to return relevant web pages and in today's social media digital world, any Tweets, Instagram or Facebook Likes that are made public. With an estimated 1.8 billion websites on the Internet today, the growth has been phenomenal since the publication of first web-page info.cern.ch by Sir Tim Berners-Lee on August 6, 1991. It's almost impossible to go through that amount of data without a search engine to look for relevancy in the information that you need. Needless to say, Google has become a dominant search engine for all Internet users, and in every one second, 68,148 Google searches (Source: Internetlivesstats.com) are being queried.

A keyword Google search of "Archimedes," the Greek mathematician famously acquainted with his cry of "Eureka!, Eureka!" when he discovered the principle of buoyancy, or simply known as the Principle of Archimedes, returns 14 million relevant pages in 0.32 seconds! From the top three relevant pages, not only that you'll know who Archimedes was but also where he was born, when was he born, whom he married to and of course the Principle of Archimedes. For those of us who are non-mathematicians, Google it and discover the mathematician in you. Not only was Google able to rank the relevant pages for you, Google also collates all the questions that had been queried by other Internet users, showing you the top few which would have been asked the most. The information one received is just endless. To add on to that, if you do a search on YouTube which is now part of the Google, you would see videos explaining Archimedes and a whole list of suggested videos on Archimedes, which you can view for free.

In other words, information, knowledge, and news are abundantly available for not just the consumers but also the other stakeholders in any organizations especially those of Fortune 500. Any form of news, tweets or information of any company, be it bad or good, fake or not, can be Googled and if the enquirer sets in the specification, more information relevant to the initial search will be pushed to him or her.

On the one hand, Fortune 500 might feel vulnerable as information could be created and shared openly by just about anyone on the Internet, but it also gives them direct access to their customers and shareholders. Companies are now able to disseminate information vital to their branding without having to wait for an intermediary media. Information such as the good sustainable projects that organizations are running in the community where they make their profits; Corporate Social Responsibility (CSR) projects, Philanthropy drive in business investments, Diversity and Inclusion practice or Ethical Sourcing initiatives which shows the positive impact any company is making to create a better future, speaks volume as compared to a well crafted Public Relationships (PR) program. Not to mention that such programs also bring about higher profits when it is made known to the world.

A quick Google search leads to an article on Fortune (2016) titled, "How Fortune's 'Change the World' Companies Profit From Doing Good" GlaxoSmithKline (GSK), a fourth-century Fortune 500 company, with a whopping US $37 billion revenue, had adopted a philanthropic business strategy of selling products with slim margins to the developing world such as India. The result is obvious, GSK made a cool profit of nearly US $16 billion in 2015 and CEO, Andrew Witty in his own words, while quoting the India market as an example, "business has gotten bigger and bigger and bigger. It makes more and more profit. And more people have access to fantastic medicines". Thus, as a consumer, one would probably gravitate to GSK's product given if a product from a rival pharmaceutical has the same efficacy because GSK is "doing good". This is especially true for the millennials, the generation born after 1980. The millennials are a growing market force, with 80 million millennials in America alone, representing a fourth of the entire population with almost US $200 billion annual purchasing power in 2015 (Forbes 2015). Some are estimating that, while this book is being written, the spending power of the millennials has surpassed all generations. And 75 percent of millennials would be loyal to companies which give back to society.

This emerging trend is also the reason as to why Fortune 500 is struggling, as the old, tried and tested way of advertisement as brand-building is not working with this group of consumers.

The openness of the Internet, easy access to information and connectivity had also disrupted many industries. Traditional industry such as hotels and taxi are two of the most obvious example, and it is of no coincidence that it is happening only now. UBER, the car-hailing startup, valued at US $72 billion today, disrupted the taxi industry globally without owning a single vehicle. In most countries, taxis are owned by large corporations which would lease the taxi back to the taxi drivers on a daily basis. Taxi drivers would have to use the first 8 to 10 fares to pay the lease before generating income for themselves. With UBER, anyone with a vehicle can make an earning without having to fork out additional cost to rent a taxi, and UBER will only make their share of income if the driver collects a fare. In a nutshell, UBER's stand is that we are in this together.

With the Internet and connectivity, hailing an UBER or for UBER to respond to a fare had also become very easy as the app enables anyone to see the proximity of the UBER car and how long it takes to get to the passengers. And once both parties had agreed on the app, the fare is guaranteed, unlike taxis whereby theirs could be down to chance.

In the case of UBER, which started in 2009, by leveraging on the Internet, information or data, it had not only disrupted a traditional industry but also built itself from a startup to billion-dollar valuation company.

Labor of Love

The onset of information superhighway had also changed the way Fortune 500's employees perceived about the company they work for and the work they are doing there. In the past, all communications even from the CEO would be first be vetted through by corporate communications to ensure hygiene factor to draw satisfaction and motivation amongst employees. Today, employees and would-be employees' access to corporate information is not only through the official channels but also independent information from consumers, Netizens, bloggers, YouTubers and much more. In a nutshell, Fortune 500 can't control the type of information that would grace the screen of their employees.

Again, while the fear of #FAKENEWS a la President Donald Trump is real, the situation also presents an opportunity for Fortune 500 to bring meaning back to work for every single employee from the senior management to the production workers on the shop floor.

Meaning of work which attests to a sense of higher purpose, whereby every employee sees their work making a difference in their community, country, and the world. If this could be done, then each employee would be able to see how their sense of purpose can be achieved by doing the work that they have been assigned to. The positive effects of achieving this would lead to engaged employees who are keen to go above and beyond the contractual terms of their jobs plus employees are who keen on developing themselves.

However, the current situation in most Fortune 500 remains much to be desired. Although every single Fortune 500 would have spelled out a vision, mission and purpose statement, these statements remain hollow to the rank and file. With 70 percent employees unable to neither remember nor recite their company's vision (Forbes 2013), it is only logical that employees are unable to relate to these "words or wordings." In their mind, these are "empty words" paid to highly expensive consultants for the purpose of branding or marketing, resulting in disengaged employees who will not perform to their potential.

What causes such disengagement when Fortune 500 today are already spending billions of dollars to train, motivate and engage their talent pool to bring about the desired business outcome for the company. We identified some of the key factors and potential mitigation possibilities:

1. A conventional economic culture approach to engaging employees. As in most business schools or management courses, employer and employees are deemed to be in a "principal-agent" relationship whereby the terms are transactional. Herein lies the problem. From this standard economic model, the agent or the employee is always deemed to be "effort-averse" as the relationship is governed in the form of a work contract. Thus for an agreed remuneration, the agent will provide a certain amount of labor, and no more. Since effort is personally costly, the agent would be unlikely to over-perform unless the principal put in more incentive or exert more control.

   Thus, to overcome the stagnation and to inspire employees to have ownership, Fortune 500 have to intersect authentic higher purpose or meaning into their business strategy and decision making whilst helping employees connect their purpose within the company. Today, employees down to frontline staff such as the production staff are able to identify the impact that they are making through the product they produce. For instance, in the past, it's near impossible for a pharmaceutical production technician to frame the asthma inhaler he or she is making into a visual greater good contribution. The production staff would only be able to see the KPI that had been handed down to him; to produce a certain amount of steroids for a certain amount of inhalers. However, today, just a search on the YouTube will allow the production technician to see the exact inhaler that he or she had produced, bringing relief to an asthma patient. These are real life videos made by actual patients, and the production team can also interact with the patients via the comments section thus bringing meaning to their daily work.

   Fortune 500 should and must capitalize on the power of the digital world to help employees "connect to their purpose."

2. Authenticity

Authenticity is merely "walking the talk." Many a time, senior management would advocate a certain purpose but if they are not behaving or perceived to be behaving accordingly, the company's vision, mission or purpose statements will ring hollow. The "principal-agent" assumption applies to senior management as well. After all, even the CEO is on a transactional relationship with the company.

So the first part is to "walk the talk," and no amount of technologies can help with that. However, the second part, to share the message and purpose with their employees, customers, shareholders, and other stakeholders, the Internet and social media provides an unparalleled platform of which CEOs of the past would envy.

One such platform is LinkedIn, a networking platform for professionals, with over 500 million users as of 2018 and of which, 40 percent of these users are active on a daily basis. What's unique about LinkedIn is that it also allows companies to create their own LinkedIn profiles and it's able to show an enquirer, who in his or her network, is working for that particular company. Thus, CEOs are able to connect with their employees via the LinkedIn platform and also potentially alumni of the company.

In the past, CEOs are hard to meet with in-person, let alone to engage them in dialogues. Via LinkedIn, CEOs are able to share not only their vision and purpose for the company but also their passion and aspirations. An example would be Sir Richard Branson of the Virgin group. He has 14 million followers, who would receive notifications of any postings or articles that he might upload to his account including those postings that he likes. Via his postings, one could see what Sir Richard cares about, and anyone can engage with him by making comments on his posting or even private messaging him. In a recent post made on his LinkedIn profile, Sir Richard shared a tree planting activity while opening the 100 Sparks of Hope Peace Park in memory of Nelson Mandela. One can infer what he cares about and how he is doing greater good via Virgin Airlines, his flagship company in South Africa.

On the same token, millennials also expect to engage with brands over social media. The key here is engagement and not just having a presence in social media. 62 percent of millennials expect engagement with brands as a basis to build loyalty and trust, and with a further 42 percent expect the engagement to lead to co-production of products for them.

Fortune 500 and the senior leadership who represents the face of the company must continuously show authenticity and in the same breath, live those values, mission, and purpose with integrity to inspire their employees to do the same.

In conclusion, to thrive in today's demand for fast, transparent and the virality of social media, Fortune 500 needs to effect a transformative organizational cultural change which incorporates the startup culture. Thus, we, the authors believe that this could be achieved by the establishment of a Department of Startup (DOS).

CHAPTER 4

Department of Startup

At the height of her powers, the sun never sets on the British Empire. In 1821, the Caledonian Mercury wrote of the British Empire, "On her dominions the sun never sets; before his evening rays leave the spires of Quebec, his morning beams have shone three hours on Port Jackson, and while sinking from the waters of Lake Superior, his eyes opens upon the Mouth of Ganges." (Wikipedia 2018)

Spanning across five continents, holding territory to the size of 35,500,000 square kilometer (13,700,000 square miles) or 24 percent of Earth's total land area, it was the largest empire in the history of humanity. By then, shy of 450 million people, would live under the policies and Governors and Viceroys out of London, so far-flung that most would have never seen or know the Kings and Queens who ruled over them. Still, all would be pledging their loyalty, and many did by involving in the wars that the British Empire found herself in and all harkens to "God Saves the Queen."

While the legacy of the British Empire still lingers profoundly today across the 53 members of the Commonwealth Nations, an intergovernmental organization of free and equal former colonies of the British Empire, not many knew that the birth of the empire, not including that of America, was sparked by the formation of a company. It was a startup, and that startup grew from a humble beginning into a colossal enterprise which gave us the Victorian Era, Britain's "Golden Years." It was a time of peace but also industrialization and world trade whereby the British Empire was the sole monopoly to the wealth of nations; tin and rubber from Malaya, spices, and tea from India, gold, and diamonds from South Africa, and ports in Singapore and much more.

The British Empire to the East which began after the loss of 13 Colonies in the American War of Independence in 1783, lasted well into the 20th Century ending only with the Handover of Hong Kong, the last colonial territory back to China in 1997. The company responsible for the British Empire second act was no other than the East India Company (EIC).

Also known as John's company, it was founded by Sir John Watts, an English merchant, ship owner and later Lord Mayor of London, on December 31st, 1600. Sir John Watts himself was a maverick; when as the owner of the ship "Margaret and John," he answered the call by the city of London in 1588 to sail against the invading Spanish Armada. John Watts himself served in "Margaret and John" as a volunteer and saw action. And again in 1590, Watts, financed privateers, private individuals who engage in maritime warfare to profit by capturing the enemy's property, in an expedition to the Spanish Mains; Spanish territories surrounding the Caribbean Sea and the Gulf of Mexico. In what is known now as "Watt's West Indies and Virginia Expedition" or the "Action of Cape Tiburon," the expedition was a success, bringing honor and significant prize money to Watts. He also earned a mention in a letter to the Spanish King when he became Lord Mayor of London in 1606–1607, as "the greatest pirate that has ever been in this kingdom".

Founded by such a colorful character of his time, weaving in the culture of risk-taking, business acumen and the correct discernment of the turn of the tides of events, it's of no wonder why the EIC lasted almost three centuries, transforming itself from a mercantile company to an empire builder.

To Venture in the Pretended Voyage to the East Indies (Startup Phase)

John Watts' initial aim in chartering the company was a modest one and that was no other than to take a bite out of the trade with the Indies, modern-day South East Asia, which had been dominated first by the Portuguese for much of the 16th century and later Dutch Companies in 1595 culminating into the formation of the United East Indies Company in 1612. He was starting from scratch and going up against incumbents who had the first mover advantage in the lucrative business. In a nutshell, Watts was launching a modern-day startup in the 1600s.

The company started with a simple statement in its charter as well, and that is "to venture in the pretended voyage to the East Indies the which it may please the Lord to prosper". The group of founders led by Watts saw an opportunity in an existing market that had already been explored by their competitors. It was a calculated risk but not an entirely risky venture that would have been left to the lady luck. Similarly today, Fortune 500 must continue to inculcate within the organization the culture of risk-taking by continuously encouraging employees to constantly ask the question "How can we do better?", to start simple yet with a strong sense of meaning and to learn from the competition. And in today's world of social media, to understand your competitors and the associated market dynamics is no longer the work of agent "Double-O-Seven" but a click of a mouse or button on a mobile device. The risk of attempting a new venture is mitigated by easy access to knowledge and information today.

Albeit founded on a simple idea of trade, the ambitious Watts presented a bigger vision to his group of co-founders, now known famously as "The Adventurers" and that is to apply for the Queen's support. Having failed initially, Watts rallied the group to reapply 12 months later whereby they succeeded in their second attempt, earning them a Royal Charter from Queen Elizabeth, giving the company a 15-year monopoly of the English trade with all countries east of Cape of Good Hope and west of Straits of Magellan. The significance of this charter is not lost to "The Adventurers", as "any traders in breach of the charter without a license from the company were liable to forfeiture of their ships and cargo (half of which went to the Crown and the other half to the company), as well as imprisonment at the royal pleasure." (Wikipedia 2018). Watts didn't want to be just "an" English mercantile sailing to the Indies, but he wanted to be "the" English mercantile sailing to the Indies.

Leaders of Fortune 500 must endeavor to share and articulate their vision for the company throughout the organization especially to those with the leadership positions. This practice is imperative not only to enable every employee to see the meaning of their daily work but also for them to make meaning out of it. In other words, leadership today is about helping employees to see the vision of the company in their meaningful way. Meaning will lead employees to look beyond the paycheck, to take extra care in their work, to put customers' benefits a top priority and to be motivated to come to work and to give their very best.

According to Guy Kawasaki, in his book, "The Art of the Start", amongst the meanings of "meaning" are:

- Make the world a better place.
- Increase the quality of life.
- Right a terrible wrong.
- Prevent the end of something good.

Helping your employees to make meaning is the most powerful motivator when the going gets tough at work and not forgetting it's also a way for them to feel valued. The programmers at Facebook would look back on the fateful day of January 14, 2011 not as day whereby they were busy maintaining the massive surge of traffic from the Middle East but how they had brought about political change to the Arab world, first by the fall of the Tunisian government and then igniting the Arab Spring. Protestors gathered in their thousands in Tahrir Square in Cairo, Egypt demanding the resignation of their president, followed by Libya, Syria, Yemen, Bahrain, Algeria, Jordan, Iraq, Kuwait, Morocco, Oman and minor protests in Lebanon, Mauritania, Saudi Arabia, Sudan, and Western Sahara.

Those at Facebook would have had no problem in answering what Guy Kawasaki had designed as a litmus test to make meaning for a startup, "if your organization had never existed, the world would be worse of because..."

Once, the Charter has been obtained and the desire to see England beat their enemy in their trade, Watts began to look for capable hands to execute the vision that he had in mind. He looked no further than Sir James Lancaster VI, a prominent Elizabethan trader, and privateer. James Lancaster was in many ways the right choice for the job. He was one of the earliest Englishmen who had set sail to the East Indies in 1591, making him an experienced hand for the job. Also, in his maiden voyage, Lancaster reached as far as the Malay Peninsula, settling in the island of Penang for three months whereby he pillaged every vessel he encountered. That made him not just an experienced sailor but also a person with the right temperament to face the challenges and the work that must be carried out as a privateer.

Watts' trust on Lancaster was rewarded when Lancaster, aboard the "Red Dragon" in EIC maiden voyage in 1601, captured 1,200 tons of Portuguese Carrack in the Malacca Straits of the Malay Peninsula. Lancaster was also able to have the foresight to trade the booty to set up two factories in Bantam, Java (modern-day Indonesia) and another in Moluccas (Spice Islands) before returning to England. These factories would later become the forward station for the empire in the East Indies. The Bantam factory would exercise authority over all the Company's factories in India and be instrumental in the founding colony of Madraspatnam, today's City of Madras. As for Watts, his vision to breach the Spanish and Portuguese monopoly had come to pass, opening a new horizon for England and her countrymen.

Talent is the key to all organization success but having talent with the right competency is only the first step. Napoleon famously said, "I prefer lucky generals." when pressed about the kind of generals he would want to serve under him. What he had really meant was that he needed not only generals who were able to execute his strategy on the field but also versatile enough to change tactics whenever the situation changed on the ground. Napoleon's generals were to be able to discern the tide of the battle and to press for advantage, which he might not have ordered, whenever an opportunity presented itself. His generals were an extension of him on the battlefield, sharing and trusting in his vision. Only then they would be able to see the right time for the right action or the right moment to seize the day. This is evident in the case of EIC, whereby in his maiden voyage for John Watts, James Lancaster was bold and forward-thinking enough to use his first booty to set up the two forward bases for the company, trusting that his decision is aligned to Watts vision and would receive his blessings.

And to achieve that, a culture of trust must be cultivated. This culture of trust is a "two-way traffic" whereby the leader first trusts the competency of the individual to carry out the task and is reciprocated by the individual trusting the strategy that has been laid by the leader. This kind of culture was found in Nokia before it became a smartphone juggernaut in the early 2000s. The Finnish Fortune 500 founded in 1855 started as a pulp mill company. Throughout its history, Nokia experimented and ventured into various industries such as papers, rubber, footwear, communication cables, military technology and even instruments used in nuclear power plants.

However, what was common as new leaders succeed the old, Nokia researchers were always encouraged to develop their projects. Nokia leaders trust that given time and freedom to explore, and their researchers will discover new invention leading to new businesses. Vice versa, the researchers trusted and shared the vision of the company. This high trust relationship bore fruit in the early 1990s when Nokia launched the first "commercially available cell phone, the Nokia 1011" (CNET 2017). From then on, Nokia continued making handphones that everyone had, building the foundation for smartphones today while growing into the world's largest mobile phone manufacturer before selling out to Microsoft for US $2.2 billion in 2002.

Although Nokia was caught with complacency and made the wrong decision in the face of new technology onslaught by Apple and Android, Nokia is already planning a comeback as we write. The culture of trust in Nokia between its leaders and talents have prevailed, allowing it to start up its mobile phone business once again.

To Make the World English

Twelve years into James Lancaster's maiden voyage for EIC, saw the company engaged their Dutch and Portuguese counterparts in a significant conflict in the Indian Ocean. The company won the Battle of Swally in Surat, India decisively, marking the EIC as a formidable naval force and masters of the sea. Dominating the seas equated to monopolizing the trades from the East and the company began to prosper.

It also ignited the company's ambition first to gain a territorial foothold and later occupy strategic territories to protect their trades. It is an innovative and ambitious approach for a mercantile company which eventually bore fruit not only for the company but also the expansion of the British Empire.

In 1612, the company requested that the British monarch, King James I to send a diplomatic mission to the Mughal Emperor Nur-ud-din Salim Jahangir seeking for a treaty giving exclusive rights to the company to reside and establish factories in Surat. The Emperor agreed when the exchange terms were to provide him with goods, valuables and precious items from Europe.

Thus began, the seed of conquest and empire building by the EIC. Trading posts in Madras (1639), Bombay (1668) and Calcutta (1690) followed. By then, in textile imports from India alone, the EIC had surpassed that of their biggest rival, the Dutch East India Company or

Vereenigde Oostindische Compagnie (VOC). VOC at the beginning of the first two decades of the 17th century was the wealthiest company in the world with 50,000 employees worldwide and a private fleet of 200 ships. EIC was only founded in the early 17th century and yet within a short 50 years, and it is beating the Goliath of its day.

One of the critical aspects of any startup is the ability to pivot its business model to a point whereby it is viable and sustainable. Many a time, startup began with an answer to a question or problem and began to build a business model around that answer. On paper, the business model may look viable, but once the startup begins to go to market, the founding team would normally discover that some of the assumptions made about the business model are not tenable. It's a critical moment for the startup as this pivoting exercise would make or break the startup. In the case of EIC, they realize very early that there will be skirmishes with their rivals and in fact, they fought at least another four Anglo-Dutch Wars after that pivotal victory in Surat.

And to secure the company's trade, it's imperative for the company to have a foothold at strategic locations for trades and military purposes. This practice marked the first pivot. EIC was then no longer just a mercantile company but a growing colonial power with dominion over territories.

By the time EIC celebrated its 70 years of foundation, King Charles II had granted the company "the rights to autonomous territorial acquisitions, to mint money, to command fortresses and troops and form alliances, to make war and peace, and to exercise both civil and criminal jurisdiction over the acquired areas" (Wikipedia 2018). The pivot exercised almost 60 years earlier had not only bore fruit but also brought the company to its pinnacle in centuries to come.

With the new mandate, the company needed to learn new skills and new talents for military conquests, administrative and policy making, ministering the economy and finances of new territories and above all to govern on behalf of the Crown. History would tell us that not only was EIC able to master these skills but also surpassed expectations in all departments, building the foundation for Britain's Imperial Century of 1815 to 1914 to the East, one and a half century later.

As a company, EIC was able to steer its employees from privateers and merchants to a proper military and governing force while not forgetting its root of a mercantile. A significant culture shift took place to enable the practices of the old of privateering to be replaced, transforming the company into a discipline, cohesive and adaptable organization. Even more remarkable, the transformation happened when the company was already a grown matured company of 70, wherein most other similar companies would have huge inertia to change. Although no one single leader has been attributed to such shift, the leaders at the helm at any one point of time in the next 150 years had maintained a culture which honored the vision and values of the company; to be risk-taking with an eye for opportunity and creativity to adapt.

This transformative-leadership not only set the vision and strategy for the company but had also transformed the company into a self-learning organization. Although building a strong army and navy was not the company's forte, but as a learning organization, EIC grew its military forces from a few hundred in the first century of its foundation to 3,000 regular troops after 1750, 26,000 by 1763, 67,000 by 1778 and reaching 260,000 in 1803; a private army that was twice the size of the British army. This growth was achieved with a smart strategy of recruiting Indian boys, and then train them to European warring capacity. Similar successes can be seen in governing; where all former colonies today adopt Parliamentary systems of governance bringing about Common Laws which allow these nations to prosper.

While having the right strategy was critical to the success of the company, its leadership realized early on that the right talent is key to success, case in point John Watts who hired James Lancaster. The company continued with this practice of hiring competent individuals to helm some of the most prominent positions in their strategic territories. One of such individual was Commander Robert Clive (1725 to 1774) whom some historians regarded as the founder of the British Empire in India. Clive joined the company as a young clerk in India for doing poorly in school. In today's standard, Clive would be a person without a degree which would condemn him to a lowly paid position in a Fortune 500. However, he found himself in a company which valued one's competency above academic excellence and helped by the fact that the company needed able men to expand its territories in India. With the decline of the Mughal Empire, the British found themselves headlong against the French in a tussle to exert influence there.

Clive proved himself a military genius, time and again with Lady Luck on his side, he turned the tables against the French with detrimental odds against him often heavily outnumbered in troops and equipment. His defining moment came in the Battle of Plassey, modern-day Palashi, situated about 150 kilometers north of Calcutta. With a force of merely 3,200 men, Clive defeated an army of "40,000 Indian and French troops, 15,000 cavalries, 50 artillery pieces and a force of war elephants" (factsanddetails.com 2013). The French never recovered from the Battle of Plassey paving the way for the British East India Company to cement their grip of India both militarily and commercially. Clive, on the other hand, became the first Governor of Bengal and with it making him a wealthy man and unprecedented profit for the company.

Many organizations, both Fortune 500 and startups alike, understand the needs for the right talent and even invest considerably in searching for these right talents. To give you an insight, Manpower, one of the top recruitment firm in the world boast an average revenue of US $19 billion per annum, servicing 400,000 clients worldwide. However, we, the authors believe that searching and recruiting the right talent with the right competency fit for the role is only the first step. The next crucial step is for the leaders of the organization to create the right culture so that these individual talents would flourish under those conditions; conditions that would bring the best out of their character, competencies, and temperament.

Startups tend to do better in that area, as many a time, they start from zero. To attract the right co-founders to form the founding team, startup founders can only sell to these talents, his or her vision for the startup, his or her leadership and the culture that they will create together in this new startup. Many a time, core founders of startups do not pay themselves and for the employees who join them, their beginning salary is lower compared to a Fortune 500. However, it is in this sort of an environment; startups build a culture that would continue to attract talents to stay and risk their careers with them. In the like of Robert Clive, he thrives in the EIC as the company recognized his potential and created a culture whereby a clerk could rise to the position of a Commander of an army. A mention of a strong founding team built on a strong culture, one would not need to look further than Paypal. Paypal was built on a simple idea to ease electronic payment replacing traditional money transfer method such as check and such. The idea was simple, but it was led by the founders and founding team who brought Paypal through the dark times of dot.com bust to a US $13 billion revenue company as of 2017. Now, infamously known as the "Paypal Mafia", had spawned three billionaires, multimillionaires and companies that are pushing innovation and forefront of technology. Notable names would be Elon Musk of TESLA, Chad Hurley and Steve Chen of YouTube and Peter Thiel of Clarium Capital who became the first outside investor to angel invest $500,000 into then the upstart Mark Zuckerberg of Facebook.

Culture: The Cry of Man in the Face of His Destiny

The success of the British East India Company, first as a fledgling mercantile company and then as a budding empire builder, shares a commonality with successful startups of our time such as Amazon, Google, Facebook, LinkedIn, and Uber. That commonality is no other than having the right startup culture, which underpins the foundation and growth of the company.

The famous French philosopher and Nobel Prize winner in Literature, Albert Camus, famously defined culture as "the cry of men in the face of their destiny" (Parker 1965). To understand Camus definition of culture, one must understand his work and philosophical thinking. Camus, in his philosophical work of "Absurdism", presented the idea of dualism such as the experience of happiness and sadness, dark and light and above all, the justification of life when ultimately mortality will conquer us all. Thus, destiny in Camus' book is of something that's meaningless like life itself, something that's fleeting with a time stamp on its expiration.

A good example would be Camus's fascination with King Sisyphus (Richardson 2011), who was punished with the destiny of rolling a boulder to the top of the hill, only for it to roll down again when it nears the top. Sisyphus would have to repeat this laborious and futile action for eternity. His destiny was a perpetual torment but yet Sisyphus, kept at it, walking down the hill and began pushing again. What drove him to continue and to push on? Can Sisyphus find happiness in the face of this absurd task?

Camus argued that by remaining lucid about his reality and simultaneously accepts and resists this reality, Sisyphus had gained superiority over his rock. Here is in Camus' words, "stronger than his rock". Although faced with eternal punishment, the punishment itself belonged solely to Sisyphus thus he remains the master of his destiny; how he would confront it. On the one hand, he understands his limits while on the other, he accepts what he cannot change and strive to the best of his ability.

Camus concludes that "this universe henceforth without a master does not seem sterile of futile to him... the struggle itself toward the summits is enough to fill the heart of man. One must imagine Sisyphus happy" (Classical Reception Journal 2012).

Therefore, we, the authors agree with Camus and opine that culture is indeed how one reacts to his or her destiny or the situation one is facing. In the case of startups, 90 percent of them according to Forbes will fail, and it's a logical outcome as all startups start with little to no cash, a small team facing established competitors, difficulty in recruiting talents and not to mention the pressure to produce in the shortest possible time. What we believe distinguished the other 10 percent is the culture which they had embraced to the face the bleak destiny of a startup. Culture is about how one refuses to despair while facing a grim situation yet finding a way out in the absence of hope. A strong culture builds the foundation of a strong organization, be it a startup or a Fortune 500.

Department of Startup: Raison D'etre

Hofstede (1980), defined culture as "a collective programming of the mind which distinguish the members of one group from another and the interactive aggregate of common characteristics that influence a human group's response to its environment".

Consequently, organizational culture would then refer to the "collective programming of the mind that distinguishes the member of one organization from the others" (Hofstede 2010). Hofstede further added that organizational culture is maintained not only "in the minds of its members but also in the minds of other stakeholders such as customer, suppliers, labor organizations, neighbors, authorities and even the press".

This organizational culture definition applies to startups aptly, as startups do possess certain unique cultural traits which are fundamental first to their survival and later their exponential growth. Furthermore, faced with a dismal survival rate, startup founders and founding team do display a set of "founders characteristics," which dictate their responses and decision making. An excellent example would be that a lot of startup founders would be willing to work for no salary to keep the startup going, especially through the difficult startup phase.

Echoing Hofstede, startup culture or "collective programming of the minds" can also be seen extended to the other stakeholders, especially their end clients or users. Apple had through the decades cultivated a following of Apple loyalists, who wait eagerly for the next Apple iPhone, iPad or Mac for their next innovative, creative design and above all, an attitude of daring to be different.

Next, what is critical about organizational culture and specifically startup culture is that it can be learned and "it derives from one's social environment" (Hofstede 2010). Once learned, it could change the mental programming of the minds of employees, helping them to thrive in today's VUCA world. And just like King Sisyphus pushing the boulder up the hill, culture is about adopting the right behavior, attitude, and values when faced with a challenge, especially a tough and "meaningless" challenge.

The question as to why do Fortune 500 need to learn or adopt a startup culture has been answered extensively in the previous chapters. The authors have also justified the need for this culture to be extrapolated to other stakeholders such as consumers, suppliers, shareholders, and Netizens. The question that begs an answer now would be what are the cultural traits of a startup for Fortune 500 to learn and adapt?

By observing the contemporary startups and that of British East India Company, one would recognize that several startup cultural traits transcended through time, applicable be it today or in the 17th century. They are, in no particular order of importance, the following:

- Calculated risk-taking.
- Keeping things simple yet big in vision and strategy.
- Make meaning daily in every single individual employee.
- Cultivation of mutual trust between leaders and followers.
- Valuing natural talents above academic excellence.

- Hiring right believers who share the company's mission on top of competencies.
- Continuous self-learning and self-development effort.
- Embracing constant change while careful of mission drift.
- Authenticity is encouraged and shown by examples.
- Grace-based leadership.

The Department of Startup raison d'etre would be to precipitate startup culture into organizations without fundamentally changing the core values of the existing organization. The key is to create a social environment whereby positive collective mental programming or in plain English, a change of mind can take place. The second reason for having a Department of Startup is to enable change on the individual level, both in their personality and human nature, when faced with an ever-changing business environment. In its purest form, the Department of Startup is neither a physical department nor a cognitive behavioral modification exercise, but a change of one's mental programming in quoting Hofstede.

In the subsequent chapters, the authors look to dive into a framework which forms the core of the Department of Startup similar to Compensation and Benefits, Recruitment, Training and Development forms the heart of the Department of Human Resource. The authors opined that the pillars of the Department of Startup are:

- Belief system
- Startup Leadership
- Followership
- Startup as a sum of all constants

CHAPTER 5

Belief System

There is only one boss—the customer. And he can fire everybody in the company from the chairman on down, simply by spending his money somewhere else.

—Sam Walton

Those words epitomized the belief system of Walmart, the first company in the history of the United States of America to generate US $500 billion in annual sales in 2017. Walmart continued to top the Fortune 500 ranking in 2018 (Fortune 2018), grabbing the top spot for the 15th time and 7th time in a row. With over 11,000 stores worldwide, Walmart employs 2.3 million employees with 1.5 million of them in the U.S. alone. Walmart is also continuously ranked as the top retailer in the world with its closest rival, Costco Wholesale Corporation coming in a distant second. According to Investopedia, the market capitalization of Walmart was US $194 billion in December 2015 versus Costco's US $73.6 billion.

Founded in the summer of 1962 by Samuel Moore Walton or better known as Sam Walton, Walmart continued to be a family-owned business as Sam Walton's family still controls over 50 percent of the company. The remarkable growth of Walmart, from a single store in Rogers, Arkansas, to the unrivaled giant of a Fortune 500, is highly attributed to the strong belief system instilled by Walton, which continued to underpin the culture of Walmart today through his family's involvement.

Walton had always put the customer first ever since his first foray into the retail business as a sales trainee with J.C. Penney in 1940. He hated having the customer to wait while he completes the necessary paperwork thus he was not one of J.C. Penney's most thorough employees. His records were haphazard and were even threatened to be fired if he didn't improve on his record keeping. On the other hand, customers loved working with him, and he added a US $25, a significant amount then to his starting salary on a monthly basis.

Walton's belief in customer service is still very much alive today. Walmart has continued to invest in improving customer service, such as customer in-store experience, by shifting stocking to daytime hours to ensure that stocks never run out from the shelf. Walmart is also sensitive to the demand of the new generation of retail shoppers who are digital natives and are looking to technology to help them save not just money, but also time.

Walmart's vice president of marketing and customer service experience Jamie Sohosky shared that Walmart acknowledges this new phenomenon and are working on helping customers save time by getting through the grocery list quicker with technology. The retail giant has immersed itself in disrupt technology from A.I., robotics to biotech to look for the technology which could bring about an impact in all layers of the shopping experience.

After the customers, Walton's second most important focus was his employees. He treated them like family and had earned their loyalty many times over. Arlene Wright who had worked for Walmart for more than 30 years since 1977, still worked as a part-time greeter at the ripe old age of 80 in 2012. She had only fond memories of Sam Walton whom she had met when he visited the stores as part of his routine. "He was such a wonderful person," Wright said.

> He was just a common man. He didn't let his success go to his head. He was very down to earth. He would ask us if we had comments, good or bad. We did get some changes made because of comments, and it could come from customers or the employees. He called us family, and he wanted everybody to be happy with how the store was run, said Arlene (Lake News Online 2012).

Sam Walton treated everyone with respect, valuing their feedback and empowered his employees to act like business owners. Employees are known as "associates" giving them both respect and a sense of ownership. "Share your profits with all your associates, and treat them as partners. In turn, they will treat you as partner, and together you will all perform beyond your wildest expectations," said Sam Walton, putting his words into action.

In 2015, Walmart raised the minimum wage for hourly associates to at least US $9 per hour, surpassing the national minimum wage by US $1.75. Chief Executive Officer, Doug McMillon, a Walmart careerist with his first role as a summer associate, unloading trucks in a distribution center in 1984 to CEO in 2014, is a firm believer in taking care of his "associates", and like Sam Walton, in sharing the company's profit with them.

In addition to the minimum wage raised which benefited 1.4 million employees, Walmart through Walmart Foundation also committed US $100 million over five years to increase entry-level workers' economic mobility and in advancing their careers, especially in the retail and service industry. "These changes will give our U.S. associates the opportunity to earn higher pay and advance in their careers," Doug McMillon, CEO of Wal-Mart Stores, said in a statement. He added, "We're pursuing a comprehensive approach that is sustainable over the long term." (Entrepreneur.com 2015).

In total, McMillon invested US $2.7 billion in associates' wages, benefits and training during a time of slow growth and increased competition from rivals such as Costco and Amazon, a strong indication that Sam Walton's belief in investing in people continues to be part of the core culture of Walmart.

The nascent Walmart which Sam Walton founded in 1962 was built on the foundation of a strong belief system which had transcended generations. It's crowning as the top Fortune 500 company is a living testimony that Walton has been right and is continuing to be right in his belief that its culture drives a strong company.

Organization Culture and Belief System

Edgar H. Schein in his book "Organizational Culture and Leadership," defined culture as a "dynamic phenomenon that surrounds us at all times, being constantly enacted and created by our interactions with others and shaped by leadership behavior, and a set of structures, routines, rules, and norms that guide and constrain behavior" (Schein 2004). In essence, Schein is accentuating the fact that leadership is about the creation and management of organizational culture. It is in his term, "two sides of the same coin."

Schein further added that culture begins with leaders imposing their belief systems; values and assumptions to the group, setting the precedence that will define not only the leadership to come in future generations but also in birthing a culture when the group is successful. This is clearly seen in the case of Sam Walton and Walmart. Walton put into practice his belief on how retail should be, avoiding the pitfalls he learned at J.C. Penny where he was declared to be unsuitable for retail business. And when Walmart began to see successes after successes, the assumptions and values began to take root, and culture is born where it inadvertently defines the organization.

Organizational culture in Schein's perspective is also evolving at all times to meet the challenges posted by the environment in which the organization operates and it's the leader's responsibility to "perceive the limitations of one's own culture and to evolve the culture adaptively" (Schein 2004). That is the essence and the ultimate challenge of being a leader and also a demonstration of the effectiveness of the culture within that organization.

Schein further developed an organizational model which consists of three levels, of which each level corresponded to how much cultural phenomenon is visible to the observer. The highest or the surface level is (i) Artifacts, which is constructed all the visible products of the group such as behavior, languages, physical environment, technologies, style, organizational structure, tradition and more. At this level, a cultural phenomenon is readily observed but difficult to decipher. A westerner may find the Japanese ritual of group morning exercises before work odd and inexplicable. (ii) Beliefs and values level, which consists of strategies, beliefs, goals or philosophies which can be observable from espoused justification. The organization's value and belief systems originally reflect that of the leader or founder, and it's adopted as the groups' shared belief when it continues to bring successes to the group in overcoming challenges. Beliefs and values at this conscious level can also predict behaviors that are seen in the artifacts level. And if these beliefs and values continue to bring successes to the group, it will be assimilated or transformed into the lowest level of "undiscussable assumptions supported by an articulated set of beliefs, norms and operational rules of behavior". (iii) Basic assumption is the lowest level, the most difficult to observe but is the ultimate source of values and beliefs. The basic assumption level is made up of unconscious, taken-for-granted beliefs, thoughts and or feelings which is the result of a high degree of consensus within the group from repeated successes in implementing certain beliefs and values. Therefore, one can understand an organization's culture by understanding the learning process by which its basic assumption comes to be.

Succinctly, it can be said that belief or belief system is the foundation of any organization's culture. Without it, the group has no compass in which to guide its response to the challenges of the environment it finds itself in. Therefore, nurturing this belief system and its underlying assumptions must be the focal point of any organizational leadership. How is that achievable? The next few sections aim to answer this question with a practical approach, implementable by the organization, its leaders and their followers.

Belief System: It Must Be True

Warren Buffett or more famously known as the "Sage" or "Oracle" of Omaha, the Founder and Chairman of Berkshire Hathaway is the world's third richest man, making the list of Forbes 400 in 2018 at the grand old age of 88 with a net worth of US $82 billion. Unbeknownst to many, Berkshire Hathaway, the investment holding company he founded in 1970, was originally a textile manufacturing company which Buffett acquired and later pivoted to what it is today. He later claimed that the textile business was one of his worst trades.

The transformation of Berkshire Hathaway from a failing textile company to the world's largest financial services company and the fourth largest conglomerate by revenue in 2018 by Forbes Global 2000, an annual ranking of the top 2,000 public companies in the world owes to Buffett's belief that his reputation and integrity (and that of Berkshire) has high economic value. Buffett guards his reputation with such immense intensity that often it went over and beyond his financial obligation to the deal at hand. This trait could be seen as early as 1972 in his acquisition of Wesco, a financial company which was about to merge with a different suitor. The CEO of Wesco, on the advice of Buffett, called off the merger at the 11th hour, causing the stock price of Wesco to fall drastically from a high of US $18 to a mere US $11. Instead of swooping in to buy Wesco at a depressed price, Buffett felt responsible for the drastic drop and to protect his and Berkshire's integrity; he started acquiring Wesco stocks at the price of US $17 before subsequently making a formal offer at US $15. The sharks of Wall Street would have disagreed with such "a colossal mistake"! Similarly, Buffett had always been willing to pay a premium for companies led by CEOs whom he deemed to be of high integrity. One of Buffett's famous quote is after all, "Honesty is a very expensive gift, don't expect it from cheap people".

Buffett's belief in integrity is also ingrained into the DNA of Berkshire Hathaway. For a financial services conglomerate with a total number of employees totaling 277,000 in 2017, Buffett had deliberately kept the department of compliance small. He believes that it is the culture of trust and personal integrity that would protect the reputation of the company and not a big compliance department.

An effective belief system which drives the culture of a company has to be adopted by the employees of the company wholeheartedly. However, to convince the rest of the employees of the company, not only that the leader of the company has to walk the talk, but he or she also has to convince the employees that they can do it too. As Buffett ceaselessly keeps himself in check to maintain high integrity in all his dealings, he simultaneously chooses to trust his subordinates that they can also lead a professional life of high integrity. Warren Buffett has clearly lived up his belief system when he said,

> The greatest institutions select very trustworthy people, and they trust them a lot. There's so much self-respect you get from being trusted and being worthy of the trust that the best compliance cultures are the ones which have this attitude of trust. This general culture of trust is what works. Berkshire hasn't had that many scandals of consequence, and I don't think we're going to get huge numbers either.

Following Schein's concept of organizational culture, a belief would be ingrained into the basic assumptions of the company, the deepest level of organizational culture, primarily when it produces empirical results. The personal wealth of Warren Buffett and the financial revenue of Berkshire

Hathaway which stood at US \$242.137 billion in 2017 had embedded the belief of integrity, trust and reputation deep into the culture of the company.

Belief System: It Must Be Communicated

Peter Drucker, the founder of modern-day management, whose writings predicted pivotal business paradigm shifts in the 20th century such as privatization, the rise of Japan as an economic power post World War II and the emergence of knowledge workers, said, "The most important thing in communication, is hearing what is not said." Therefore, communication must not only speak to the mind but also the heart.

As a belief system is foremost about winning the hearts of a group of individuals, effective communication is a must. The most significant responsibility lies with the leader or the leadership of the organization. The leader must become the belief or value that the organization is espousing to be. He must show that he is living and breathing the belief system, moving hearts and minds to join him through his actions. Warren Buffett, who is also renowned for his belief in giving back to the society, communicated that belief through his philanthropic work. He had promised to donate away 99 percent of his wealth and had to date, donated a whopping US \$35 billion to charities and foundations such as the Bill and Melinda Gates Foundation. Action not only speaks louder than words, but also a convincing and robust communication tool.

Another form of communication will be to encourage employees to visualize the positive aspects of adopting the belief system, or conversely, the consequences of neglecting it. However, the key is to lead each employee to visualize it at his or her level. The positive impact or the negative consequences must be felt at their own personal capacity. Again, Warren Buffett had demonstrated that he knows how to reach to each and everyone's heart and to get them to live his belief of integrity at the workplace through his "newspaper test". Written in the Berkshire Hathaway Inc. Code of Business Conduct and Ethics handbook, employees are urged to fall back on the newspaper test whenever they are in doubt or when they find themselves in ethically ambiguous situations. Buffett's rule of thumb is,

...I want employees to ask themselves whether they are willing to have any contemplated act appear the next day on the front page of their local paper to be read by their spouses, children and friends-with reporting done by an informed and critical reporter (Berkshirehathaway.com 2018).

Through a simple example, Buffett had communicated a lasting impression about ethics to his employees.

Lastly, for any belief system to be wholeheartedly adopted by employees or any group of individuals within an organization, it must be communicated to them at their level of understanding. Leaders must meet every individual and speak their "language" to win hearts and minds. A case in point would be Warren Buffett's annual shareholder letter. Buffett's famous annual letters are filled with stories, quotes, witty comments on investments, leadership, ways to value shareholders and employees, management decision, but above all, he is communicating his beliefs to the shareholders in their language. In one of his letters, he simply said, "It's insane to risk what you have and need in order to obtain what you don't need" (Berkshirehathaway.com 2018). That simple sentence epitomize Buffett's investment beliefs which had brought him and Berkshire successes after successes, that is, investing for the long-term and not to be perturbed by short-term losses. Concurrently, the language use is a simple everyday mantra in a small shareholder's household whereby being prudent with expenses is practiced on a daily basis.

Buffett's annual shareholder letters are a popular feature which is highly anticipated by everyone, including Wall Street bankers, since he wrote the first one in 1965.

Belief System: It Must Be Evolving and Increasing

Culture is a pattern of shared basic assumptions that was learned by a group as it solved its problems of external adaptation and internal integration, that had worked well enough to be considered valid and, therefore, to be taught to new members as the correct way to perceive, think, and feel in relation to those problems.

—Edgar H. Schein

From the formal definition of culture defined by Schein earlier, culture is formed due to the fundamental human need for cognitive stability, consistency, and meaning. Culture allows the group to maintain those needs for stability by providing a form of appropriate response that would make sense in overcoming the external challenges. In Schein's three-layered model of organizational culture, this proven "cognitive defense mechanism" would be basic underlying assumptions which define to the group what to pay attention to, how to define issues or situations, how to react and what possible actions that may be appropriate and so forth. In its essence, these underlying assumptions are the DNA of the group which would help to guide the group to thrive, bringing cohesion to the group, especially in assimilating new members. One can catch a glimpse of the manifestation of these basic assumptions at the beliefs and values level in the form of how the group justifies their actions.

Conversely, these basic assumptions could also be detrimental to the group when some of the elements of the assumptions are no longer valid, or have become dysfunctional due to the changing environment. The changes could be due to the introduction of new technologies such as artificial intelligence, the emergence of new consumer behaviors in the form of millennials, or as simple as a merger and acquisition. It is precisely at this moment when cultural change needs to be initiated, that the same characteristics of basic assumptions which had been instrumental to the group's survival, became a double-edged sword that could scupper it.

To change something that has been universally agreed by the group as "truth" would bring about cognitive instability, anxiety and emotional distress to the group. The next natural thing to happen is for the group to fall back on what's familiar to them and to perceive the new situation as congruent with their assumptions. This model explains why some CEO and companies had continued to ignore what's "written on the wall" and didn't take the necessary action to evolve, as demanded by the changing business environment. A case in point would be Kodak, the camera film-making company, when it ignored the emergence of digital cameras.

As such, beliefs and the deeper layer of basic assumptions besides that of ethical elements, would need to evolve as the environment facing the group evolves. Such evolution may not necessarily be of something negative, but to take advantage of what the new environment has to offer.

In this sense, the responsibility lies with the leader of the group or company. Leadership in Schein's opinion is about deciphering what elements within the organizational culture that has become dysfunctional, and to initiate the necessary changes. Schein identified the keys to a successful culture change as (1) management of anxiety that would occur from the relearning of basic assumptions and subsequently change in beliefs system and (2) to assess if the gene for new learning is present with the current group.

One practical approach that has been greatly underutilized is the concept of mentoring. Mentoring provides an excellent platform for the more seasoned member of the group or employees to share the basic assumptions of the organization with new members. New hires need time and mentoring to comprehend the underlying assumptions to the values and beliefs that are taught to them during the orientation week. For new members, having a mentor would also allow them to question the underlying assumptions against what they bring to the group thus bringing clarity to why the group reacted differently to a similar situation they might have encountered previously. This channel for informal questioning is highly critical as it will open up a common ground for the mentor and the mentee to share openly about their assumptions when they are working together toward a challenge, a fundamental experience to forming culture. And conceivably through the shared experience, success would follow, leading to a shared assumption as "the power of culture comes about through the fact that assumptions are shared and, therefore, mutually reinforced" (Schein 2004).

Another benefit of mentoring is that it can also help provide the necessary feedback to the leadership via the mentees on the changing external challenges. Jack Welsh, understood this very well by starting the concept of "reverse mentoring" in General Electric (GE), whereby the roles of the mentors and mentees are reversed. Young recruits who are more technology inclined are given the role to mentor the management who are of the older generation, thus less technology competent. Today, the former is known as "digital natives" and with the rapid changes in the digital world, reverse mentoring is a welcomed program.

In conclusion, organizational culture is ultimately made up of individuals who had chosen to align themselves into a group, sharing experiences, learning, and assumptions. However, they are individuals with different roles within the organization such as a leader or a follower or even stakeholders such as shareholders, customers, and vendors. The authors believe that one needs to see the organization through cultural lenses which examine the individuals in the role that they are in within the organization. Henceforth, in the later chapters of the book, the belief system of a leader, a follower and the company would be examined in respect of a startup founder, startup core employees and the startup itself.

CHAPTER 6

Startup Leadership

Acceptance Is Bliss

As the Founding Father, the first Vice President and the Second President of the United States of America, John Adams, was also instrumental in selecting the Committee of Five, charged with drafting the Declaration of Independence. Adams chose himself, Thomas Jefferson, Benjamin Franklin, Robert R. Livingston, and Roger Sherman but it was his decision later that would forever seal his leadership legacy and statesmanship in the history of the United States of America. Adams persuaded the committee to choose Jefferson to draft the document although it is well known that Jefferson is a weaker debater compared to him. This fact was later corroborated by Jefferson when he hailed Adams as "the pillar of the Declaration's support on the floor of the Congress, its ablest advocate and defender against the multifarious assaults it encountered" (Wikipedia 2018).

Jefferson's thought, from the very beginning, was that Adams should be the one drafting the Declaration and he pressed Adams to do it. In the recorded exchanges between these two statesmen, Adams gave three reasons for declining Jefferson.

Jefferson is a Virginian, and he believed that a Virginian ought to appear at the head of this business, as another Virginian Richard Henry Lee presented the first formal proposal for independence.

Adams gave authority to where authority belongs. He greatly respected the fact that the idea of independence sprouted from a Virginian, and he wanted the recognition to be given where it is due. A startup leader does not seek the recognition that is undue of him but goes above and beyond to recognize the contribution of his fledgling team members to instill ownership, giving power and authority over their work.

"I am obnoxious, suspected and unpopular. You are very much otherwise," Adams gave his second reason to Jefferson.

Adams had accepted who he was and wasn't pretentious in trying to be someone he was not. He knew his limitations and chose another person whom he deemed was better than him, stronger than him in writing the declaration although it would also mean that the recognition will go to Jefferson as the Principal Author of the Declaration of Independence. A startup leader acts the same and surrounds himself with co-founders who share the same belief as he does but stronger in other areas, complimenting him to grow the startup.

"You can write 10 times better than I can." Adams third reasoning.

While acknowledging that Jefferson was a better author than he was, Adams was also able to impress upon Jefferson, his confidence and trust in him to carry out the task. The impact was automatically felt when Jefferson replied, "Well, if you are decided, I will do as well as I can." A good leader is not only able to recognize talents in others but also to trust and be authentic when delegating to team members who possess the required talents. In a startup, due to the lack of resource and talents, its leader needs to trust the talents that have gathered around him and be authentic about that trust. With that, the startup can grow exponentially and thrive in the fashion of the fledgling United States of America of July 4th, 1776.

Therefore, the first requirement for a successful startup leader is the ability to accept and be comfortable with who he or she is. Acceptance is a liberating act, allowing the leader to anchor himself, leading to self-confidence and later to self-assurance. A leader who is self-assured is highly critical to creating a startup culture as he would not be afraid to bring in smarter people than he is. Steve Jobs, a classic example of a self-assured leader, once said, "It doesn't make sense to hire smart people and tell them what to do; we hire smart people so they can tell us what to do." Only with such a leader, a smart and robust founding team can be built upon and for the startup to grow in winning the market or producing the next breakthrough technology.

Also, acceptance of one's weaknesses would lead to humility and further on, to valuing and respecting people. Only a leader who can accept that there are things that he can't do but others can; then he can see value on those talents and not the cost of employment. And it is a universal truth that people who feel valued are those who would be the most loyal, most productive and most likely to stay the longest.

One of the positive outcomes of valuing employees is the respect that you will have for them. It's a natural transformation whereby when you appreciate someone, you will tend to respect them. Georgetown University's Christine Porath surveyed about 20,000 employees worldwide, and respondents ranked respect as the most essential leadership behavior. To quote from Kristie Rogers, in her article, "Do Your Employees Feel Respected? Show Workers They're Valued, and Your Business Will Flourish", "Employees who say they feel respected are more satisfied with their jobs and more grateful for—and loyal to—their companies. They are more resilient, cooperate more with others, perform better and more creatively, and more likely to take direction from their leaders" (Harvard Business Review 2018). Thus, the benefits of having a respectful culture where every employee felt valued are enormous and must be pursued diligently by every leader. That journey, however, begins with the first step of accepting oneself as a leader for who he or she is.

Be the Giant for Others to Stand On

On May12, 1780, a short four years after declaring independence from the British, John Adams wrote a letter to his beautiful wife, Abigail, from Paris. While he was admiring the beauty of Paris with visits to Gardens of the Palais Royal, the Gardens of the Tuileries and more which he described to Abigail, he lamented that it was something which he should have done 25 years ago. Instead, he had exchanged a peaceful and blissful life with "my Head is too full of Schemes and my Heart of Anxiety" to give birth to a new nation, a new hope for Americans.

Adams further added that it was something that he had to do and the reason he gave would allude to his beliefs that a leader must not only be a visionary but also one with a servantship heart.

"I must study politics and war that my sons may have the liberty to study mathematics and philosophy. My sons ought to study mathematics and philosophy, geography, natural history, naval architecture, navigation, commerce, and agriculture, in order to give their children a right to study painting, poetry, music, architecture, statuary, tapestry and porcelain" (John Adams May 12, 1780).

In Adams' vision of a new America, he was leaving an inheritance to generations of Americans to come, not just for his lifetime. He was building a country with his fellow compatriots that will give sons and sons of America to come, a chance for peace, opportunity to prosper and wealth of choices. The America that we know today, a country leading in startup and technology innovations is built on that vision, giving it a strong foundation to overcome adversity and to reinvent itself time and time again.

Adams did not stand on the shoulders of any giant, but he became the giant for generations of Americans to stand on. His vision was not only for a better America but also one which will transcend generations. His vision had also given birth to generations of American leaders who through their self-sacrifice and service became giants of their own rights.

The key is to have a self-belief system which anchors on service to others, self-sacrificing but yet not without its reward and to be patient while waiting for the fruits of one's labor to show. Jeff Bezos of Amazon, the second company in the world to hit a market capitalization of US $1 trillion, shares the same belief. Amazon under his leadership since its inception in 1994 has now, on September 4th, 2018, joined Apple in the only two companies reaching the trillion dollar milestone, beating the combined market capitalization of Exxon Mobil, Procter & Gamble, and AT&T. Furthermore, Amazon's revenue has now surpassed that of the economic outputs of countries such as Hungary and Kuwait (CNBC 2018). Jeff Bezos, undoubtedly is the wealthiest man in the world today with a personal wealth of approximately US $166 billion, with Bill Gates coming in a distant second with US $70 billion short.

What was Jeff Bezos' belief that drove him and Amazon, which started in his garage, to its unprecedented success today? Bezos had three simple beliefs: put the customer first, invent and be patient (8 percent.com 2017).

Put the customer first—servicing others and in this case customers. Bezos had made it a point time and again that Amazon should obsess over its customers and not competitors.

Invent—Bezos famously said that, "Failure and invention are insep-
arable twins. To invent you have to experiment, and if you know in
advance that it is going to work, it is not an experiment." In other words,
failure is not only tolerated but also celebrated in Amazon to allow Bezos
to create "new giants" in his company every day. He is willing to sacrifice
the company's bottom line to enable his fellow employees to push the
boundaries of their potential and advertently that of Amazon.

Be patient—Bezos had repeatedly stressed on this point, that the
key is to think long-term which ultimately requires a lot of patience.
Evidently, this was also spelled out clearly in the Amazons Leadership
Principle—"They think long term and don't sacrifice long-term value for
short-term results."

And just like Adams, Bezos is also building an inheritance that would
transcend time and for the benefits of Americans and citizens of the world
long after his passing. Bezos had envisioned his latest startup Blue Origin,
founded in the year 2000, to colonize the solar system in time to protect
humanity in the face of an impending self-inflicted demise.

If ever this book is read by someone in Mars in light years to come,
that seed was sowed by no other than the visionary, Jeff Bezos of Amazon,
born in Albuquerque, New Mexico on January 12th, 1964.

Leadership Minus 1

"A soldier will fight long and hard for a piece of colored ribbon," a leadership mantra by the famous Napoleon Bonaparte of Corsica on how
proper reward and recognition has an astounding effect on the soldiers he
led. By giving the credit they so deserved, Napoleon had inspired his men
to trust their lives for a piece of ribbon which carries an insignificant price
but of priceless honor and recognition.

At the battle of Lodi on May 10, 1796 during the Italian campaign,
Napoleon, then a young commander of the French army led his men in
pursuit of the retreating Austrian army of the Habsburg Monarchy to
the Bridge of Lodi. Fortified across the bridge were a battery of cannon
threatening to destroy any force who dares to attempt to cross. Backed by
nine battalions of infantry, arrayed in two lines, the French would have

first to brave the cannon fire, then the muskets of the Austrian men with no more than 10 yards of breath to maneuver. The French carabineer (elite light infantry) with great courage, stormed the bridge and took it in a single attack. At one point, when the offense was wavering due to heavy casualty, senior officers rushed to the front and led the attack again. The French won the Battle of Lodi with 1,000 casualties versus 3,200 enemies killed with a further 2,000 captured. Napoleon was generous with his recognition.

In his letter to the French directory, Napoleon wrote, "If we have lost few men, this fortunate circumstance is due to the prompt execution and the sudden effect produced on the enemy's forces by the immense masses rushing forward, and likewise of the dreadful fire of our invisible column. Were I called upon the designate the soldiers who have distinguished themselves in this battle, I should be obliged to name every carabineer of the advanced guard and nearly all the staff-officers" (Romantic Circles 2018).

Napoleon understood the heart of men. It is the personal recognition that inspired and motivated his men to face the volley of fires and certain death. Every individual desires recognition according to Maslow's 5 Level Hierarchy of Needs (Maslow 1943). Maslow theorized, once an individual satisfies the lowest level of needs, he would be motivated to satisfy the next level of needs. In the 5 level Hierarchy of Needs, the lowest level comprises of physiological and safety needs also known as basic needs, followed by psychological needs; belonging and self-esteem needs and finally the need for self-actualization whereby one needs to achieve his or her full potential as human beings.

Self-esteem, which is placed at the second top level, is a form of needs whereby individuals sense a need to accomplish something and for that accomplishment to be recognized. Individuals need to feel that they are valued by others to build their self-esteem and also basked in the prestige that comes with that recognition. It is innate in us, the strong desire for recognition and we are motivated to fulfill that need even it is of little material value.

And, by giving recognition where it is due, one is not only helping the individual fulfill his need for self-esteem but also the other psychological need for belonging. The need for belonging or social acceptance is an emotional need, and it would drive human behavior to fulfill it. Recognition is a form of testimony that the individual is accepted into the social group and strong emotional ties will be built to the group.

Furthermore, in research conducted by The Gallup Organization in 1999, employees' engagement and motivation were found to be strongly affected by how often they receive recognition for their work. Thus, it is imperative for organizations to build a recognition culture and to be specific about the frequency of this recognition. Christina Bielaszka-DuVernay in her article, "Are You Using Recognition Effectively." with Harvard Business Review, suggested one every other week as a guideline. However, the frequency should be dependent on the individuals that made up the organization and managers should make it a point to find that out.

In a startup, recognition is easily given as it is a flat organization. One's contribution is easy to be noticed in a startup, and after that, to provide an award as recognition. However, in a Fortune 500, recognition system becomes complex. Often, employees are demoralized as they felt that their immediate supervisor or line manager would covet their contribution for personal recognition. This is especially so for functions that are not easily measured quantitatively such as customer service or accounting. Recognition now becomes counterproductive, creating distrust and disengagement.

How would then Fortune 500 create a fair, accurate and sustainable recognition system and culture in such diverse markets and a large number of employees?

We advocate the concept of "Leadership minus 1" as a more sustainable recognition formula that could permeate all levels, all culture, and all employees. The basis to this concept is for managers to focus their recognition and reward to the next lower level of reports, skipping their immediate direct reports. The managers' immediate direct reports would then be recognized by their superior instead. The concept of "minus 1" is to get leaders to look into recognizing employees one level lower, bringing transparency to the reward system albeit with some rules and conditions. A simple illustration would be for the Director of Operations to give recognition to the work of Operations Supervisors (Minus 1) while the Operations Manager (direct report) recognizes the work of the Operations Technicians.

The current practice of managers providing the recognition for the work of his direct report and for his direct report to reciprocate the recognition and reward system to his charges has contributed to one major issue; mistrust in management, boss, team, and colleague. In a global survey conducted by Ernst & Young on the issue of trust in the workplace, less than half of the 9,800 full time working respondents have a "great deal of trust" in their current employers, bosses, and colleagues (EY 2016). This phenomenon is seen across national culture, in a variety of companies in Brazil, China, Germany, India, Japan, Mexico, the UK, and the U.S. Ernst & Young also found out that the top factors for lack of trust in employers (management) are unfairness in compensation and unequal opportunity for pay and promotion while the reason for lack of trust in bosses (direct manager) are bosses not providing recognition for a job well done and lack of transparent communication. All factors point to a single root problem, and that's a broken recognition and reward system.

"Leadership Minus 1" aims to overcome these challenges and to create a culture of high trust within the organization via recognition. What then constitutes the building blocks of this concept?

Concept:
Leaders to recognize and reward the work of one level lower reports instead of direct reports.

Conditions:

1. The organization must be explicit about the trust that they have placed in their leaders to the leaders' direct report.
   For example, in a manufacturing environment, the Director of Production must take all measures to convey to the Production staff, his trust in the Production Manager to perform to expectation.
2. Project goals or performance expectations of leaders must be made clear to their direct report.
   The Director of Production must also detail out the Production Manager's performance expectations to the Production Staff. And in the process of explaining that to the staff, the Director must show how their personal performances influence the outcome of the Manager's performance.

3. A clear message must be sent out to the leaders' direct reportees that their utmost urgent matter is to perform at their work to meet this leader's performance expectation.

It's imperative that the Director emphasizes that the Production Staff most important daily goal is to meet the Manager's performance expectation through their work.

4. The reportees recognition and reward are reciprocal to their responses to the Manager's leadership.

The reward albeit comes from the Director is reciprocal of the Production Staff's working toward meeting the Manager's goals. Their responses to that determine the reward that they will receive. To further illustrate, the Manager may be expected to reduce a certain amount of wastage, and the individual who finds innovative solutions to significantly reduces wastage at his station will be rewarded and recognized by the Director.

Benefits:

1. Effective recognition and reward allowing better engaged and motivated employees. This also results in lower turnover rate. A study by Bersin and Associates (Forbes 2013), showed that companies with ample employee recognition have 31 percent lower voluntary turnover rate than companies that don't.

2. Effective informal succession planning program whereby direct reports are encouraged to work toward the competencies and skills required for the next level of position, in this case, the Production Manager.

3. Increase transparency in the reward system promoting trust amongst the employee, the management and the leaders in question.

4. Empowering leaders, as the direct reports' reward are wholly dependent on working toward their leader's goal. This is also an informal conveyance of trust that the company had put on the leader.

Leadership Developer

Jean Lannes, one of the staff officers who rushed forward to lead the attack again at the Bridge of Lodi when it began to waiver, was Napoleon's most daring and talented general. Made a Marshall of the Empire with titles of 1st Duc de Montebello and Prince de Siewierz, he was also a personal friend to the Emperor. Napoleon wept when the Marshall was mortally wounded at the Battle of Aspern-Essling, whereby he bore the amputation of one of his legs with great courage. Marshal Jean Lannes, was later interred at the Pantheon National, as a recognition of his distinguished service to France.

What is little known is that Jean Lannes joined Napoleon's French Armée d'Italie, as a simple volunteer, fighting and distinguishing himself up the ranks. Napoleon was spot on with his remark on Lannes, "I found him a pygmy and left him a giant."

From a lowly infantryman to a brigade general, to the commandant of the consular guard, to the Marshall of the Empire and finally as the ambassador to Portugal, Napoleon was instrumental in Lannes's career. Napoleon understood very well the potential beheld by Lance and grew him into those positions with trust.

One of the fundamental strength of a startup leader is his ability to understand his people and to help them maximize their potential as good talents who are willing to throw their lot with a fledgling startup. While startup leaders may not have the inkling of an organizational psychologist but merely striving to slow down the cash burn rate by hiring the right "lesser" people, they may have found the best motivational technique for their employees.

Sitting at the pinnacle of Maslow's Hierarchy of Needs is the need for self-actualization. Maslow defined self-actualization as "the desire for self-fulfillment, namely the tendency for him (the individual) to become actualized to his full potential. This tendency might be phrased as the desire to become more and more what one is, to become everything that one is capable of becoming" (Maslow 1943). Maslow believed that every human has an inborn desire to self-actualize. Thus, leaders who see, understand and work toward "self-actualizing" his reportees, is motivating and building leaders of tomorrow. In the case of Paypal Mafia, the 14 original employees under Peter Thiel, (who sold PayPal to eBay for US $1.5 billion in 2002) went on to create seven different unicorns with a total net value of roughly US $75 billion in 2015.

However, to be able to do that, leaders need to know the potential of their team members like the back of their hands. And one of the best ways to achieve that is to measure it with psychometric tools such as ability tests and personality questionnaires coupled with the performance at work. Personality questionnaires are in effect behavioral assessment with an output on one's competencies, measuring it as either strength or weakness. As competency is a series of behavioral traits which leads to the desired outcome, such as leadership or strategic thinking, leaders are able to work with their team members on the area of potential (strength) and to start building a team which could uplift each other (weakness).

Nonetheless, psychometric tools must not be the only source of information in identifying potentials. Performances are another indication on the potentials be held by employees especially through the "Leadership minus 1" concept whereby employees are constantly rewarded for helping to reach not their own goals but of their manager's, thus showing them the competencies required for the next level role.

Last but not least, is to create a culture of self-discovery, allowing employees space and time to consider their potentials and to weigh in on how they can become the best possible person they are meant to be. The key here is to allow self-discovery henceforth the exercise must also encompass life outside of work. Who they are naturally.

An area that could allude to more information to help employees "self-actualize" is no other than their hobbies. Everyone would have a hobby which they strive to improve themselves to a new level of mastery or in other words to be the best they can be. This process of iteration allows the employee to understand himself better and it can be translated back to work in the form of a self-motivated employee. Hobbies also may help companies discover new hidden talents, abilities, and skills set.

"Know yourself and you will win all battles", a famous quote by Sun Tzu, a military strategist of the six century B.C. and author of the book "The Art of War," summarizes aptly the importance of understanding oneself as even in war, it is the key to victory. Therefore, it is imperative for leaders to help their employees to do just that.

CHAPTER 7

The Follower

Self-Sacrifice

On a cold Friday morning of January 20, 1961, at the eastern portico of the United States Capitol, in Washington, America swore in her youngest and one the most charismatic leader she has ever seen—President John F. Kennedy. Following a narrow victory over Richard Nixon, an 8-year incumbent Vice President, Kennedy, a war hero and a Pulitzer Prize winner delivered an inauguration speech of hope, strength, compassion and the belief in the power of Americans working together.

The crowd lauded Kennedy when he threw the challenge to his fellow Americans to a lifetime commitment toward public service for the greater good. Americans, young and old, harkened to Kennedy when he said, "Ask not what your country can do for you but what you can do for your country." Those words inspired a whole generation of young Americans to embrace the idea of self-sacrifice and to volunteer to help the more impoverished populations in America and the world. Many joined the Peace Corps, a volunteer program initiated by President Kennedy himself to bring about social and economic development abroad in Third World countries while promoting a mutual understanding between America and the country served. Peace Corps produced many renown alumni, and in the startup and technology world, Reed Hastings, the co-founder of Netflix would need no further introduction.

Reed Hastings volunteered in 1983 to 1985, teaching mathematics in Swaziland, Africa and he chose Peace Corps "out of a combination of service and adventure" (Inc.com 2005). Hastings attributed his entrepreneurial skills development, especially the appetite for risk-taking, to his time spent there. In an interview with Matthew Boyle of Fortune in 2007, Hastings had this to say, "But once you have hitchhiked across Africa with 10 bucks in your pocket, starting a business doesn't seem too intimidating" (CNN Money 2007). With the seed planted in Africa, Hasting founded his first company Pure Software in 1991, bringing it public in 4 years before it was acquired.

Spotting an opportunity when he had an overdue fee for the "Apollo 13" video cassette which he had misplaced, Hastings started Netflix, fully admitting that he wasn't sure if the customers would come. Netflix changed the way we view television and home movies. It brought about a culture of on-demand movies whereby you can choose to watch your favorite movie, anytime, anywhere. In 2013, Hastings took another risky plunge by getting Netflix to produce its very own television series, "House of Cards" starring Kevin Spacey which went on to win 3 Emmy awards. Today, Netflix has a market capitalization of US $152 billion as of May 2018, with 125 million subscribers in more than 190 countries (Fortune 2018), streaming movies, drama, cartoons to all computers, laptops, smartphones and more. Hasting himself, has a personal net worth of US $3.7 billion (Fortune 2018) and true to his humility, he had attributed it all to serendipity.

Through service to others and self-sacrifice, one is poised to reap the seeds that one has sown and in abundance. One of that seed is self-discovery. The process of self-discovery will open one's heart to what is important to him, what he is capable of and what is his "self-actualization" need is. Reed Hastings has in his volunteering role, discovered that he has the risk appetite to be an entrepreneur and doing business was something that is important to him. That changed Hastings, who holds a Masters in Computer Science from the University of Stanford, from choosing a path as a computer scientist to a startup entrepreneur.

Lao Tzu, an ancient Chinese philosopher, and writer of the 4th Century B.C. once said, "He who knows others is wise; he who knows himself is enlightened." Hastings is the best example of an enlightened soul and where it took him still surprises him till today.

Startup employees who are willing to put in the extra hour, the new initiative, the enthusiasm to learn from mistakes would be likely to find his "enlightened self," who he is, his potential and his competencies. Accordingly, it is of utmost importance for Fortune 500 with active Corporate Social Responsibility (SCR) program, to be more deliberate in helping employees who volunteered to begin the process of self-discovery. The benefits are tremendous especially when employees are able to discover their "self-actualization" needs or their true vocation while serving others. Here, self-actualization could be something that one is passionate about. Passion is most often found in something that one is competent in or potentially competent in. Motivated, purpose-driven and passionate employees will do wonders in their work.

Vice versa, employees or followers must take an active role in the process of self-discovery while volunteering their time. Volunteering can be within the company's CSR program or with selected Non-Governmental Organizations (NGO), Foundations or Charities of their choosing. The choice of a cause to volunteer or in what capacity should one be involved in is not as critical as getting started and participating actively in one. Because it is while doing the volunteering work, one would begin the discovery process.

However, one should take the initiative to be mindful of what stirs his heart while performing these services. Some of the key questions that one could pose to themselves are:

- What are the joys that I can draw from volunteering?
- Do I feel peaceful and loved while I am working in this capacity?
- What are the elements of this servanthood that brings about kindness and goodness in me?
- Where have I found the patience and faithfulness in me to carry on the work when it began to look insurmountable?
- How often have I been able to be gentle and to exercise self-control while volunteering when in a normal situation at work, I would have reacted differently?

Being deliberate and truthful in one's answers to the previous questions not only would help tremendously in the discovery of one's passion, but above all, one's real potential or vocation. In Frederick Buechner's own words, "Vocation is where your greatest passion meets the world's greatest need."

Trust to Be Trusted

The current employer-employee relationship is one bound by contract, a transactional one. For a certain amount of time of the day or a certain amount of labor, the employee would be remunerated in an agreeable amount of reward. As much as such arrangement has brought about significant protection to the employee and also to the employer, it has however damaged the mutual trust among the two parties.

In the words of controversial labor lawyer Sir Otto Kahn-Freund,

> The relation between an employer and an isolated employee or worker is typically a relation between a bearer of power and one who is not a bearer of power. In its inception it is an act of submission, in its operation, it is a condition of subordination.

In Otto Kahn-Freund's argument, he views the need for the State to be one of the elements in the tripartite industrial relations with Employer and Employee, albeit as an abstentionist. Interference from the State is only as a last resort.

It is of little wonder that trusting their employer is of little value to employees. In a global survey conducted by KarynTwaronite of Ernst & Young in 2016, fewer than half of the surveyed professionals have high trust in their companies. A further 15 percent of the surveyed 9,800 employees, age 19 to 68 from Brazil, China, Germany, India, Mexico, Japan, the UK, and the U.S. reported "very little trust" or "no trust at all". And with today's practice of "hiring and firing", a norm in the employment market, Kahn-Freund's rather negative taking on the trust level between these two parties still hold water today. Trust is found wanting to the point that he sees a need for the introduction of labor law albeit adopting more of a "laissez-faire" attitude.

Albeit against the backdrop of such unequal relationship, it is however still in the best interest of employees and followers to first give their employers their trust. Ernest Hemingway put it best when he said, "The best way to find out if you can trust somebody is to trust them." Nevertheless, by first taking the first step toward trusting one's employer or leader, one is not only creating an opportunity for a transformational relationship but also satisfying his Maslow's need for security and safety. Once the need for security has been met, one can then work toward creating an emotional relationship to build a sense of belonging and social security within the organization.

The trust which in its essence is a form of confidence, bold and secure or action based on that security, forms the crux of any relationship. Hence, by first extending trust to others, one is taking the first step in a relationship, and allowing the other party to know you better. And by building on that relationship, mutual trust can be established. One has to give out trust to earn trust.

Trusting others is a matter of mindset while trustworthiness is a product of behaviors. In other words, when someone chooses to trust, he or she would likely to have a change of heart which would lead to actions or behaviors that would build on that relationship. These behaviors, stemming from a trusting heart would then be seen and acknowledged as trustworthiness.

Most startup employees, especially for startups in their infancy, adopt a trust first policy when they choose to join the startup founder instead of a more stable career with a Fortune 500. Many of their peers might have thought they had chosen to do in blind faith, but in actual fact they had decided to trust not only the founder but also what the startup stands for and how both the founder and the startup are aligned to their self-belief system.

Craig Silverstein was Google Employee Number 3, after the co-founders, Larry Page, and Sergey Brin. He was the first person employed by Page and Brin after having studied together with them at Stanford University for his PhD. Silverstein's contribution to the building blocks of Google is legendary amongst Google. In Page's own words, Silverstein's codes were instrumental in the success of Google today. A Harvard graduate as well, he was also admitted to the Phi Beta Kappa, the oldest and most prestigious honor society in America, honoring outstanding liberal arts and science students. He had plenty of choices to work with the top 1 percent of the Fortune 500, but instead, he chose to trust his fellow students, Larry Page, Sergey Brin, and Google.

What drove Silverstein to put his trust in Google and its founders so early in the startup phase? Google then was just an idea in a dorm room in the halls of Stanford.

The answer was crystal clear in Silverstein's goodbye e-mail to the staff in Google when he left in the year 2012 to join Khan Academy. Silverstein had this to say for his 13 years in Google,

> While a lot has changed at Google over the years, I think we've done a remarkable job of staying true to our core mission of making the world a better place by making information more accessible and useful. I am looking forward to pursuing that same mission, though in a slightly different way, at Khan.

Craig Silverstein had trusted Google, Larry Page, and Sergey Brin that their belief system matches that of his; to make the world a better place by making information accessible and useful. Google and its founder had reciprocated that trust and stayed true to their values and belief system. In his final parting words, Silverstein again emphasized how Google's belief system had affected him to choose Google, and he wrote "When I write my massive 4-volume autobiography, "Craig Silverstein: the Man Behind the Legend," I will devote an entire volume to my years at Google. I can't emphasize enough how meaningful my time at Google has been, and how meaningful all of you have been to it."

Throughout his time with Google, Silverstein was trusted, and is seen by many, as the third founder. His reward was not only in recognition but also monetarily. From his tenure with Google, his only employer to date, Silverstein had amassed a total of US $950 million in remuneration.

Trust to be trusted is a truth that is as old as the hills, and those hills stretch all the way back to the time of Lao Tzu in the 4th century B.C. in one of his famous quote, "He who does not trust enough will not be trusted."

Be Teachable and Learn

As we approach the cusp of the 4th Industrial Revolution, skills acquired in the previous century or even those that are just 10 years ago could have been obsolete. Technology, automation, artificial intelligence, big data, and smart machines had continuously changed the landscape of the job market and at a rate that is unprecedented. Some had even challenged the relevance of traditional universities especially in the field of technology. In 2013, Dr. Carl Benedikt Frey and Professor Michael Osborne of the Oxford Martin School published their seminal paper, "The Future of Employment: How Susceptible Are Jobs to Computerisation," whereby they predicted that 47 percent of jobs in the U.S. are at risk of automation. Their study is based on the argument that one can predict the future of jobs by just observing what the computers or technology are capable of doing. And in their estimates, they had examined the susceptibility of 702 occupations which comprise 97 percent of the U.S. workforce and compared that to emerging technologies such as artificial intelligence and automation. The conclusion Frey and Osborne had, was a sobering one, they had been somewhat conservative with the 47 percent prediction, and the world of work is changing again and at a faster pace. We, the society as a whole, from leaders to educators and ourselves need to respond appropriately.

American philosopher, author, and teacher of spiritual, psychological growth, Vernon Howard said,

> It is a mistake for anyone to think he has lived too long in his old, unsatisfactory ways to make the great change. If you switch on the light in a dark room, it makes no difference how long it was dark because the light will still shine. Be teachable. That is the whole secret.

Howard had in so little words described both the nascent predicament and its solution for the 21st century careerist. The answer lies in being teachable. Are you teachable? Are you humble enough to be taught? Would you be willing to accept that learning will be lifelong as technology continues to evolve? Would you be willing to allow someone half your age to teach you?

Disruption to skills and jobs in the 21st century is no longer a hypothesis but a reality. Jenny Soffel, Digital Lead from the Centre for the Fourth Industrial Revolution, World Economic Forum, mentioned emphatically that "the gap between the skills people learn and the skills people need is becoming obvious, as traditional learning falls short of equipping students with the knowledge they need to thrive". She further alluded that for job candidates to thrive in the Fourth Industrial Revolution, they would need to be able to collaborate, communicate and solve problems, skills developed through what is known as social and emotional learning (SEL). Although traditional skills are still necessary, it is imperative for the 21st-century careerist to be proficient socially and emotionally.

The clear and present message is that lifelong learning is the new norm. One could not, and must not, end their learning once they have earned their degrees or even post-graduate degrees. The evolution of the digital economy is disrupting even the most traditional industry such as business and finance. Monzo became the first United Kingdom online-only bank to obtain a full banking license since its inception in 2015. In a short span of just three years, it had attracted already 500,000 customers with all transactions done online or via an app. The United Kingdom Financial Services Compensation Scheme (FSCS) had already agreed to cover deposits up to the amount of £85,000. The new dawn is here.

As the argument for the need is laid to rest, the toughest yet is the question of how can one adopt a teachable mentality. What are the challenges or the obstacles from making one teachable?

Elizabeth Bennet, the protagonist in Jane Austen's best selling romantic novel, "Pride and Prejudice," almost forfeited her true love when her prejudice swayed her away from Mr. Fitzwilliam Darcy while Mr. Darcy himself was guilty of the same due to his pride.

While prejudice has a preconceived opinion that is not based on actual reality, pride is having too high an opinion of what is real of oneself. Both are stumbling block to a teachable heart.

Pride, if left unchecked, would lead to a "know-it-all" mentality with no room for new learning, as one may say that, you can't add more to an already filled cup. In this rapid digital advancement age, it is very likely "teachers" would be the Millennials (those born in the 80s) and the Generation Z (born 1995 onwards) who are digital natives. To be taught or to learn from a younger generation requires one to humble oneself and to keep an open mind to learn. There must be a renewal of mind that "teachers" of the 21st century may not come with long years of research work or titles of a well-read university academician.

Reverse mentoring, a concept first popularized by ex-GE Chairman Jack Welsh, whereby more senior executives are mentored by younger employees who are digital natives in areas of technology and social media, is increasingly becoming a critical part of Fortune 500 developmental needs. The benefits are astronomical as Fortune 500 would be able to use resources which are hired at the entry level to bring employees and leadership team up to speed in the technology trend with curated content. Also, the pace of change is so fast that traditional training especially classroom type of training are rendered ineffective. Alan Webber, the co-founder of Fast Company, put it best when he explains about reverse mentoring,

> It's a situation where the old fogies in an organization realize that by the time you're in your forties and fifties, you're not in touch with the future the same way the young 20-somethings. They come with fresh eyes, open minds and instant links to the technology of our future (Forbes 2011).

Prejudice, on the other hand, would breed the "nothing-to-learn" mentality. Being judgmental rob ones of the opportunity to learn, as it had stifled the sense of curiosity. Nothing is worthy of learning. It may also lead to stereotyping whereby one uses mental "files" to process new information by comparing them to past knowledge and experiences. The biggest problem with that is the knowledge from even just a year ago may already be obsolete in the fast-changing digital economy.

Mumbai Dabbawalas (lunchbox delivery men) is a 5,000 strong force with an average class 8 literacy, elementary school education in Indian standard delivers over 130,000 lunch boxes throughout Mumbai in a day, bringing home-cooked food to the customers and returning the empty dabbas (metal lunch box) the same day. Stefan Tomke from Harvard Business Review estimated that,

> Every working day they transport more than 130,000 lunch boxes throughout Mumbai, the world's fourth-most-populous city. That entails conducting upwards of 260,000 transactions in six hours each day, six days a week, 52 weeks a year (minus holidays) but mistakes are sporadic.

The speed and accuracy of the Dabbawalas were made even more impressive with the fact that they didn't employ any form of technology, not even a cell phone.

These semi-illiterate individuals had impressed Harvard Business School not only to publish a case study on them but also to give them a "Six Sigma" grading which means that the Dabbawalas made less than 3.4 mistakes per million transactions (BBC 2017). Naturally, Fortune 500 such as FedEx and Sir Richard Branson of Virgin Airlines are some of the notable companies who had spent time learning from them.

Lastly, the top 10 skills in 2020 identified by the World Economic Forum in its Future of Jobs Report, are:

- Complex Problem Solving
- Critical Thinking
- Creativity
- People Management
- Coordinating with Others
- Emotional Intelligence
- Judgment and Decision Making
- Service Orientation
- Negotiation
- Cognitive Flexibility

One can deduce from the prior list that being prideful or prejudicial would hinder the acquisition of most of the skills which are paramount to being successful in the 21st century.

Find Your Destiny

Dwight David Eisenhower, or popularly known amongst his fighting men as "Ike," was the Supreme Commander of the Allied Forces in Europe during World War II. In post-war America, Eisenhower was elected to be the 34th President of the United States of America. One of his famous quotes was the one mentioned in the TIME magazine on October 6th 1952, "Neither a wise man or a brave man lies down the tracks of history to wait for the train of the future to run over him".

One's destiny lies within his or her own free will, and it is one's prerogative to make the best possible decision for oneself.

Netflix was forefront in putting Ike's words to practice as an organization as a whole, with emphasis on freedom and responsibility as one of its core culture. Netflix describes this rare responsible person as someone who embodies the following behaviors:

- Self-motivating
- Self-aware
- Self-disciplined
- Self-improving
- Acts like a leader
- Doesn't wait to be told what to do
- Picks up the trash lying on the floor

And it's Netflix firm believe that by giving and increasing this freedom, it will continue to attract and nourish innovative people to help the business sustain successes in the rapidly changing economy.

In the same breath, this "rare" employee is expected to be responsible for his or her career path including pay and promotion. Netflix even allows their employees to compare what they are being paid to the global market. True to its words, Netflix shuns the traditional and formalized development program but instead creates the necessary environment and opportunities for high performing employee to self-develop, by "self-improving through experience, observation, introspection, reading and discussion" (Netflix.com 2018). Career management is a personal responsibility and not "planned" by the company.

Anna Eleanor Roosevelt, the wife of President D. Roosevelt, also the longest-serving First Lady of the United States of America, has this to say about freedom,

Freedom makes a huge requirement of every human being. With freedom comes responsibility. For the person who is unwilling to grow up, the person who does not want to carry his own weight, this is a frightening prospect.

Now if one has been weighed and found to be adequate, what's then the best path to discover one's destiny or vocation. How does one discover his or her destiny? Where can the discovery process begin? The pathway perhaps lies in not searching for a particular job or career, but to search for a position and the impact it will have on society.

It may be easier for startup employees to define and relate to the said position as the startup has the advantage of starting from the very beginning, which is describing the good it wants to do in the society. In the case of Google, the good for the society is freeing the reign on information, making it accessible and useful to the masses. The impact of any positions within Google to the society can be easily defined as it is about empowerment from politics, health to finding your way with the Google map during your holidays.

However, if one is to seek a position within a Fortune 500, the same thought process must take place although it might take a little more effort to recognize it due to the complexity of a Fortune 500 business. All in all the position must provide both extrinsic values in terms of remuneration and its intrinsic value: it is good in itself. The work that comes from the position must be intrinsically good first to self, loved ones, society and the world in general.

Ultimately, the position should lead to one's destiny or vocation, and it should fulfill three dimensions outlined by Greg Ogden:

- The individual experience an inner oughtness
- It is bigger than the individual
- It brings great satisfaction and joy to the individual

CHAPTER 8

Sums of All Constants

People First

On October 10th, 2018, Amazon, the e-commerce giant made a surprising announcement in scrapping its AI recruiting tool, bucking the trend of using AI in the hiring process. With a global headcount of 575,700 and rising, it's only logical that the Human Resources (HR) in Amazon pursues AI as the solution to a faster, more efficient and robust talent acquisition process. AI has been hailed as the holy grail amongst HR practitioners whereby AI would be able to process the thousands of job applications data, regurgitate them and produce in ranking the top 5 must hire candidates. In the case of Amazon, similar to the "recommendation list" or the "inspired by your shopping trend."

Amazon's algorithm, however, pulled the wool over their eyes when it consistently showed disdain against women candidates. Amazon's AI was displaying a temperament of a six-year-old boy who typically exhibits the "I don't like girls" syndrome. The algorithm had failed at the fundamental function it meant to do, to bring in the best talent for the job objectively.

In its effort to create a more robust and fair selection system, Amazon automated the selection process of software developer and technical position by training its AI neural networks with data of resumes submitted over ten years. Based on those 10-year data, Amazon expected its AI to rank candidates in a one to five stars ranking and to be gender neutral in those ranking. Unfortunately, for the past ten years and even today, the technology industry is still a predominantly male-dominated sector causing the AI to learn this aspect as part of its selection algorithm. This was despite the massive effort to ensure that neutrality is maintained; 500 computer models, focusing on specific job functions were created with each model trained (machine learning) to recognize close to 50,000 terms that showed up on past candidates' resumes and to assign significance to all skills. Much to the chagrin of the Amazon team, the computer models "favored candidates who described themselves with verbs that are commonly found on male engineers' resumes, such as 'executed' and 'captured'" (Reuters 2018).

Despite the massive popularity of AI in recruitment with the likes of Goldman Sachs and Hilton pursuing similar technology to aid hiring process, Amazon made the bold move to scrap its AI recruiting tool as it had shown that it was discriminating against women. Although Amazon had taken considerably care when the system first showed signs of such biases by editing the AI program, there was no guarantee that the trained machine will not device new ways to discriminate women. Therefore, Amazon pulled the plug on its AI selection to remain consistent to its belief system, to be fair and gender neutral in its selection for the best person for the job.

Amazon's phenomenal growth to being the second largest employer in the United States of America can be traced to Jeff Bezos' obsession with what he termed as "high standard culture" whereby Amazon sought to retain the highest possible standard in all areas of their work.

Bezos' further explained in his 2017 Annual Report letter to shareholders that,

A culture of high standards is protective of all the 'invisible' but crucial work that goes on in every company. I'm talking about the work that no one sees. The work that gets done when no one is watching. In a high standards culture, doing that work well is its reward—it's part of what it means to be a professional.

Scrapping the AI recruitment tool, is part of this invisible work and readily admitting that the technology does more harm than good, is being professional. Amazon is to be commended for being consistent in its approach to the AI recruitment tool.

In a survey conducted by workplace insights platform kununu.com in 2018, Amazon rated higher than the US average in all but 5 of 18 categories with Gender Equality and Diversity being the top two categories. On a scale of one to five, Amazon scored a 3.99 versus a 3.90 US average for Gender Equality while Diversity obtained a score of 3.96 against the average of 3.71. These ratings are nods of approval from current Amazon employees when they are asked to compare their current view of the company as compared to two years ago. Again, it is evident that Amazon has been consistent with its belief system, hiring the best talent for the job regardless of gender or ethnicity.

As technology takes center place in our workplace, it is imperative that companies continue to put people first in all its decision-making process. Christian Lous Lange, a Norwegian political scientist, historian, and Nobel Peace Prize winner in 1921 put it aptly when he said, "Technology is a useful servant but a dangerous master." Lange was also the foremost proponent of the theory and practices of internationalism, and his work of Histoire de l'internationalisme was widely accepted as the basis for the formation of League of Nations post World War I. He was often called upon with issues regarding disarmament and arbitration.

Although we do not live in Lange's turbulence time, technology can still be a dangerous master if we become subservient to it. The best illustration of that scenario will be if Amazon decides to continue to use its AI in candidate selection when it has critically shown that it is detrimental to job seekers specifically and the society in general. Companies must continue to ask the pertinent question: how adoption in any form of technology will still put its people first? People here being its employees, customers, shareholders, the society and the world in general.

Renewal of the Minds

Up to the 16th century, the cradle of learning and inventions had always been the Far East. Notably, China was one of this cradle with her Four Great Inventions namely the compass (206 B.C.), gunpowder (1044 A.D.), paper (100 B.C.) and printing (206 B.C. to 220 A.D.), stretching back to the early centuries of civilization. These inventions lifted humankind to a new era of intellect, communications, history, politics, state of socio-economy and above all prosperity. The Four Great Inventions were also instrumental in the development of a new capitalism Europe in the later centuries, creating empires and colonies which spanned the world with the British Empire being the biggest.

After the Chinese, then came the Islamic Golden Age, dating from the 8th to the 14th century, which saw the explosion of science, knowledge, economic and cultural works. The contribution of the Islamic Golden Age, especially in the area of science, mathematics, geometry, physics, chemistry, pharmacies are still evident until today. One notable discovery is in optics through the work of Alhazen (HasanIbn al-Haytham), the modern "Father of Modern Optics." Alhazen was the first to correctly argue that vision occurs when lights, traveling in straight lines, reflect off an object into the eyes. And the common knowledge today that vision occurs in the brain rather than in the eyes is also the discovery of Alhazen.

The question that begs an answer is why the "Great Enrichment," the prosperous modern age which started in the 16th century till today did not occur in Beijing or Baghdad but instead in London, Paris, and Rotterdam? How did Europe overtake the centuries of intellectual work and prowess of the east?

While the Far East was cultivating a culture of intellect pursuit, cultivating scholars of all fields, Europe was still obsessed with the learned ways of the old. Classical learning of ancient Greek scholars Aristotle, Galen, Ptolemy and more, dominated the learning culture of Europe to the point of restricting intellectual growth. "As late as 1580, an Oxford don could be fined five shillings for teaching something that was contradictory to the writings of Aristotle" (Mokyr 2017). The belief system of that time in Europe is that the truths or facts have been revealed to humankind through the classical text and to challenge these truths are heresy.

It took several mavericks such as Robert Boyle of Boyle's Law, the modern astronomer Tycho Brahe and the polymath Paracelsus to kickstart a new era of discovery and innovation by initiating a transformative cultural change in learning science and technology. In short, these "modern" scientists seek to challenge the underlying belief system in Europe especially amongst the intellectual circles on the issue of science and technology. "Driven by new observations and information, intellectuals ripped to shreds the classical texts in physics and medicine, and subjugated them to what they believe to be persuasive evidence and logic" (Mokyr 2017). Now, every theory or hypothesis must be backed by evidence either through observation or logic. Science discovery must be evidence-based. With the new culture of learning, Europe embarked on a modern age of prosperity which lasted till today.

Similarly, companies today are enamored with short-term, quarterly financial performances to the point of sacrificing the company's long-term growth. Public listed companies are put under higher scrutiny with quarterly announcements affecting its share prices, directly impacting the value of the company. Under such condition, it is only natural for companies to pursue less risk-taking in strategy, making incremental innovation and some might start lowering quality to increase profit margins. And in that process, companies began to lose the values that first made it great.

In the quest for profits, companies began to adopt unethical practices that harm not only the clients but the company's image itself. Even the mighty Apple had indulged in questionable practices of slowing down older iPhones to compensate for decaying batteries thus forcing clients to upgrade to newer models. Wells Fargo's, the fourth largest bank in the U.S. by total assets of US $1,870 billion was mired by scandal after scandal in 2017. Wells Fargo admitted that it had charged up to 570,000 consumers for auto insurance that they didn't need and consequently repossessing 20,000 of vehicles. Further adding to Wells Fargo's woe was an admission of the creation of a total of 3.5 million fake accounts without consumers' permission to inflate financial results.

According to the Edelman Trust Barometer, the world has entered a trust crisis in 2017. The general population trust in four key institutions that were measured namely; business, government, NGOs and media has declined across the board, a first since they were being tracked in 2012. Trust in business dropped to 52 percent globally, just 2 percent shy from the tipping point of distrust. 13 countries, amongst them G7 nations such as Japan, United Kingdom, and Germany had earned the dreaded title of "distrusted."

There is an evident need for a paradigm shift in the current practices of companies putting profits first or for them to be measured that way. A new cultural transformation such as that experienced by the learned scholars of the pre "Golden Enrichment" must occur, otherwise businesses will face the consequence that befell the East. Companies must go back to the fundamental reason of their existence which is to serve society and serve they must, by prioritizing people that form those societies.

In a global survey done by The Economist in February 2018, Josselyn Simpson of the Intelligence Unit found out that young innovators and entrepreneurs are placing greater emphasis and growing importance to social responsibility. 70 percent of these young entrepreneurs say that it is more important to be socially responsible now compared to five years ago and a further 66 percent agree that social responsibility is essential to business success. And the areas that they care about passionately are education, social justice, and equality. Fortune 500 has a learning lesson here with these young Turks who are turning around the concept of business on its head. They also believe that there is a trade-off if they pursue social responsibility first and they are agreeable with that trade-off. Not contented only to have this belief within their startups, these young entrepreneurs and innovators also want customers and potential customers to know their values and belief system.

Fundamentally, the objective of any startups is to impact lives, and the founder's belief system is to make the world a better place, believing if they do that first, the market will reciprocate. Increasingly, the market is beginning to sync with this belief. In the same survey, The Economist found out that 60 percent of consumers will buy a product or a service from a socially responsible company even if it costs more. The millennials, as discussed in the earlier chapter, are most likely to form part of this group of consumers. Millennials, also known as Generation Y is by far the largest generation with more than 70 million individuals in the United States of America alone. With such large representation and its ensuing spending power, "Millennials are at present the most influential and promising consumer and promising group in shaping the modern world" (Lifehack 2018). Millennials believe in shaping the world in their spending habits, choosing to buy from socially responsible company bringing positive change to the world.

The message is clear. Companies are now required not just to be seen in putting aside some budget for a CSR program but would to start using its business as a force for good. B Lab, a non-profit organization, started by Jay Coen Gilbert, Bart Houlahan and Andrew Kassoy in 2006 dedicates itself in harnessing the power of business for good, to solve social and environmental problems in society. B Lab provides an overall impact assessment of a company on its operation and business impact to its employees, community, environment, and customers, leading to a B Corporation or B Corp certification if all standards are met. A certified B

Corp certified companies gain trust from the consumers as it is verified to have "meet the highest standards of verified social and environmental performance, public transparency, and legal accountability to balance profit and purpose" (BCorporation.net 2018). The concept of B Corp continues to grow, and it begins to see more prominent organizations such as Patagonia the American clothing giant joining its rank.

Concurrently, a handful number of Fortune 500 which had heeded this new phenomenon and began to focus on their Corporate Responsibility Program (CSR) and sustainability program have also shown the positive progressive result in winning over consumers especially millennials. Fortune 500 such as Unilever, Coca-Cola, PepsiCo, AT&T, and IKEA had successfully employed social media and online channels to communicate their environmental and social sustainability program effectively, winning consumers especially the social media savvy millennials.

The market is renewing its expectation of a company, measuring it against standards that do not put profit above social responsibility thus it is wise for Fortune 500 and businesses alike to start responding to that demand.

Speak My Language

"If you talk to a man in a language he understands, that goes to his head. If you talk to him in his language that goes to his heart," a famous quote by Nelson Mandela, the son of a Xhosa-speaking Tempu chief, who brought to an end the apartheid South Africa and becoming its first black president. Perhaps what that made him truly great was when released from 26 years of political imprisonment, he was greeted rapturously by both black and white South African. He became a reconciliatory factor for the new nation, putting hate aside and by speaking in a language that harkens not only to a South African's head but also his or her heart.

As much as languages are building blocks to communication, it is above all a window to culture. Communication happens when a common language is spoken, but real connection only takes place when one speaks in the "culture" of which that language commands. Language is a crucial component of cultural identity and with it the function of communicating values, belief system, and tradition. To speak to someone's heart is to acknowledge his or her belief system, values, and customs and to draw common ground from the depth of these manifestations of culture. This "language" is what Mandela alluded.

Language is an intrinsic component of culture, and scholars such as Hofstede and Brewster have widely acknowledged that. In Hofstede's "Dimensions of National Cultures," language is a good gauge of the dimension of individualism versus collectivism (IDV) whereby the index explores if one society is more favorable toward the interest of an individual over a collective group or vice versa. In a nutshell that would be if the "I" is bigger than the "we", or the other way round. Yoshi and Emiko Kashima, the former a psychologist while the latter a linguist, studied the relationship between language and culture through the concept of pronoun drop, the omission of the singular pronoun "I" from a sentence. They found through a sample of thirty-nine languages in seventy-one countries that in an individualistic culture (e.g., United States of America), the language spoken would require the speaker to use the pronoun "I" while it is dropped when it is a language spoken in a collective culture (e.g., Japan).

Language is also part of a culture that can be learned which modifies the human nature (e.g., fear, anger) of a particular group of society. Thus, human nature such as fear or anger which is universal could be expressed differently in a different society. Japanese tends to be known to be a good listener, and if one is to observe a Japanese conversation, one could not help to wonder in awe on how patient the listener is, keeping quiet with a slight nod of acknowledgment and responding only when the speaker has finished. Apart from the fact that the Japanese society places a high premium on politeness, unbeknownst to many, the Japanese language is designed with the "verb" being placed last in a sentence. A typical example of an English sentence would be, "I go to school" but in Japanese, it would be "School I go" with the singular pronoun "I" being omitted in a conversation. What essentially has happened is that the listener would have to listen all the way to the end to know what the speaker intends to do, either he or she intends to go to school or otherwise. Henceforth, Japanese might find it rather rude if they are interrupted midway in their speech when they speak in English, the lingua franca of the world, as it is not culturally done in their native language.

Similarly, many found it odd for Koreans to ask for their age in their first meeting when most individuals, especially of the fairer sex, would instead like to keep it a secret. The reason is that culturally Koreans is a highly hierarchical society where one is accorded respect due to their seniority. The Korean language has built-in titles for each depending on his or her standing in the hierarchy corresponding to the speaker. Needless to say, there are formal speeches which are reserved for someone higher in the hierarchy.

Henceforth, the fastest and most effective way for any individuals to understand a new culture of a new market is to learn its language.

In today's connected world, where businesses, Fortune 500 and start-ups alike operate in multiple countries, understanding culture is a "must have." To err in that area had proven to be costly such as the failed merger of Daimler (German) and Chrysler (American) of the late 1990s which ended with losses and layoffs. The clash of culture resulted in Daimler selling off Chrysler to Cerberus Capital Management in 2007 for US $6 billion when it had paid US $37 billion for Chrysler nine years earlier.

Startups face a similar dilemma today but at a quicker pace, as many a time startups focus on a niche market and often that niche market is too small domestically. Startups are forced to look at similar niche markets overseas early on its growth trajectory.

Fortune 500 and startups alike must begin to take language learning for its employees seriously to thrive in today's global market. "Think global, act local" anchors on a strong foundation of cultural understanding and that begins with learning the local languages. If there were only one training program required, it would be language courses.

However, companies should take a broader approach and not restrict its employees to learn languages where it intends to do business in but to allow employees a freehand to learn any languages of their choosing. An employee learning any foreign language is good as it helps them to open up their mind and to gain a new perspective in business communication. Additionally, psychologists have also found that speaking a foreign language improves one's cognitive ability by challenging one's brain to recognize, make sense and to communicate in a different language system.

Lastly, The University of Chicago has also found that bilinguals are able to make more rational decisions as they tend to use their second language to reconfirm decisions made in their native language to avoid biases, prejudices, and nuances which may slow down their decision-making process.

Hire by Culture

In their final day of lecture, in spring of 2010, Harvard Business School graduating class asked HBS Professor Clay Christensen to address them on how to apply the business theories that they had learned from him in their personal life and career. Professor Clay Christensen proposed three questions to be answered, and they are (1) How can I be sure that I'll be happy in my career? (2) How can I be sure that my relationships with my spouse and my family become an enduring source of happiness? And the last one (3) How can I be sure I'll stay out of jail. Though the last question seems to be distant for most of us and even more so for highly intelligent individuals such as a graduating class of Harvard Business School, Professor Christensen was quicked to put that to rest with evidence. Two of his 32 Rhodes scholar classmates spent time in jail, and Jeff Skilling of Enron was a classmate from Harvard Business School.

For all of the aforementioned questions, Professor Christensen applied business theories but underlying these theories were the need to build the right culture. And in some cases, hiring the right culture.

The answer to the first two questions lies with deliberately designing desired values and behaviors into an organization's or family's culture and allow it to evolve voluntarily. Employees and children alike build desired behaviors such as self-esteem by trying over and over again at tasks and learning what works from it.

As for the third question, the answer is found within oneself. Do you have within yourself the integrity and moral compass that would keep you out of jail? Professor Christensen advocates building a culture within oneself that avoids the "Marginal Costs" mistake. Marginal Costs model points to a practice in finance and economics whereby one is taught to evaluate alternative investments by looking solely at the marginal costs and marginal revenue each alternative provides. The decision should ignore all the other aspects such as fixed costs or sunk costs. When applied to the question of how do I stay out of jail (how do I live a life of integrity), often one would employ the marginal cost model when choosing between right and wrong. In Professor Christensen's own words, he explained the concept marginal cost of "just this once."

> A voice in our head says 'Look, I know that as a general rule, most people shouldn't do this. But in this particular extenuating circumstance, just this once, it's OK.' The marginal cost of doing something wrong 'just this once' always seems alluringly low. It suckers you in, and you don't ever look at where that path ultimately is headed and at the full costs that the choice entails. Justification for infidelity and dishonesty in all their manifestations lies in the marginal cost economics of 'just this once' (Harvard Business Review 2010).

The current practice of hiring focuses on the "right fit for the job." Candidates are typically assessed via competency matching to find the best fit candidate who will be successful on the job. These competencies are derived from the assessment on one's abilities, behavioral profiling, and skills acquired from education or work experiences. On the other hand, each job would have its own set of competency profiling, and a typical "best fit" candidate would have a high competency matching ratio. This practice of competency matching or competency assessment has its merits as it is very useful in selecting a candidate with a strong aptitude to excel in the job. However, it had ignored the candidate as an individual and put the focus on the job. It had overlooked the culture of the candidate, and the subsequent cultural fit to the team and organization.

A company or an organization is built up of people, and the culture that is inherent in the person and the team is highly critical in moving the company ahead to reach its goals. Thus, the current practice of hiring must prioritize the candidate and not the job. The practice of hiring by culture should be given much more weight over the hiring on job fit.

Angel investors invest at the very early stages of startups when they are also at the riskiest. Often the startup would be burning cash to build the business with no clear sight of breaking even, and most startups would not survive. However, angels investors are continuing to invest, and almost certainly, most angel investors invest in the founder of the startup and not the startup per se. A good angel investor would prefer to dive deeper into the founder and his or her co-founders instead of the business plan. "Pivoting" an action of changing the course of the business model frequently happens in the startup, but the founder and the founding team remains constant. It is in them the angel investors put their trust—the culture within the founder and the founding team; how the team works on the difficulties they face, to overcome them and to build consensus together. Edgar Schein described this process as the fundamental mechanism of building a culture. With experiences of successes, the team would begin to embrace priorities and act with instincts when faced with challenges. That in any sense, in the authors' opinion include the amalgamation of personal culture into the team.

The next question that begs an answer would be what is then the anatomy of hiring by culture?

First and foremost, companies should present a clear picture of what transformative change any candidate can expect if they choose to join them. The current job profiling on which the job description is based on, focuses on the present self of the individual candidate. Almost all job descriptions demand years of experience in a specific area before the candidate is being considered, but none share the potential growth and transformative change the candidate will experience while working on the job. If an organization is looking to break into a new market or an innovative change, it might be profitable to hire someone with no experience but with the qualities of exploration, adventure, curiosity, and perseverance.

Secondly, companies must become who they want to hire. By building the desired culture within the organization first, the right candidate with the right cultural fit will be attracted to apply. According to Schein, organizational culture is made up of three levels layered on top of each other; (i) artifacts which visible, readily observable but could be hard to interpret. Artifacts' cultural elements include behaviors, traditions, products, languages and such. (ii) values and beliefs which consist of elements such as values, justification, mindset, the cognitive process, that are less observable but could be inferred from how employees justify their actions. (iii) underlying assumptions, the foundation of culture which is so widely shared that many are not aware of it. The cultural elements are assumptions, ideologies, philosophy, worldview, ethics, thinking and such. To design and to bring about a desired organizational change, companies must set out to understand the underlying assumptions that are driving the company. Once that is completed, the outward change would be noticeable to the outer world through the top layer of artifacts.

Last but not least, is the focus on values and beliefs in the selection and recruitment process with an understanding of the national culture of the candidate. The use of psychometric assessments such as personality or behavior questionnaire continues to be a good guide, but measurement should be made to focus on behaviors that distill the right values. Whereas aptitude, skills, and experience ought to take lesser weightage in consideration of the candidate where possible.

The ultimate aim is to understand the candidate's basic assumption of his or her values and belief system. That can be further derived from the interview process by learning from the candidate's experiences in overcoming difficulties, challenges at work and what the candidate perceived to be the "best" way to meet his destiny; quoting Albert Camus.

Hiring is not about poaching the top talent from a rival, but to find a good match to the company. Startups continue to rely on this to attract top talent by promising not material gains but appealing to the belief system or the culture of the individual candidate.

References

All Things D. 2012. "End of an Era: Google's Very First Employee, Craig Silverstein-Technically, No.3-Leaving." available at http://allthingsd.com/20120209/googles-very-first-employee-craig-silverstein-technically-no-3-leaving/

American Enterprise Institute. 2017. "Fortune 500 Firms 1955 vs. 2017: Only 60 Remain: Thanks to The Creative Destruction That Fuels Economic Prosperity." available at http://aei.org/publication/fortune-500-firms-1955-v-2017-only-12-remain-thanks-to-the-creative-destruction-that-fuels-economic-prosperity/

B Corporation. 2018. "Certified B Corp." available at https://bcorporation.net/certification

BBC. 2017. "The 125-Year-Old Network That Feeds Mumbai." available at http://bbc.com/future/story/20170114-the-125-year-old-network-that-keeps-mumbai-going

Beaumont, P. 1992. "The US Human Resource Management Literature: A Review." In *Human Resource Strategies*, ed. G. Salaman. London: Sage.

Beer, M., B. Spector, P. Lawrence, D. Mills, and R. Walton. 1985. *Human Resource Management: A General Manager's Perspective*. New York, NY: Free Press.

Berkshire Hathaway. 2018. "Berkshire Hathaway." available at http://berkshirehathaway.com/

Business Insider. 2018. ""Economic Blackmail": Zara, Qantas, Marriott and Delta Airlines Reverse Position on Taiwan for Fear of Angering China." available at http://businessinsider.com/zara-marriott-qantas-apologized-to-china-listing-taiwan-as-country-2018-1

Business Insider. 2018. "Jeff Bezos Says Amazon is Not His "most important work" It's This Secretive Rocket Company That Toils in The Texas Desert." available at http://businessinsider.com/jeff-bezos-blue-origin-rocket-company-most-important-2018-4

Chief Executive. 2018. "United Airlines CEO Oscar Munoz's Off the Mark Management." available at https://chiefexecutive.net/united-airlines-ceo-oscar-munozs-off-mark-management/

CNBC. 2017. "5 Key Business Lessons From Amazon's Jeff Bezos." available at https://cnbc.com/2016/05/13/5-key-business-lessons-from-amazons-jeff-bezos.html

CNBC. 2018. "Here's How Amazon's $1 trillion Market Cap Stacks Up Against the Rest of the S&P 500." available at https://cnbc.com/2018/09/04/heres-how-amazons-1-trillion-market-cap-stacks-up-against-the-rest-of-the-sp-500.html

CNET. 2017. "How Nokia Made The Modern Cell Phone." available at https://cnet.com/news/six-things-nokia-did-to-make-the-modern-cell-phone/

CNN Money. 2007. "Daimler pays to Dump Chrysler." available at https://money.cnn.com/2007/05/14/news/companies/chrysler_sale/

CNN Money. 2007. "Questions For ... Reed Hastings." available at https://money.cnn.com/magazines/fortune/fortune_archive/2007/05/28/100034248/index.htm?section=money_latest

Consumer Goods Technology. 2016. "Walmart Plots the Future Customer Experience." available at https://consumergoods.com/walmart-plots-future-customer-experience

Edelman. 2017. "2017 Eldeman Trust Barometer." available at https://edelman.com/research/2017-edelman-trust-barometer

Entrepreneur. 2015. "Wal-Mart to Spend $1 Billion Raising Employee Pay to at Least $9 an Hour." available at https://entrepreneur.com/article/243113

Ernst & Young. 2016. "Global Study: Could Trust Cost You a Generation of Talent?" available at https://ey.com/gl/en/about-us/our-people-and-culture/ey-global-study-trust-in-the-workplace

Facts and Details. 2015. "Britain, the Raj and the East India Company." available at http://factsanddetails.com/india/History/sub7_1d/entry-4121.html

FINN. 2018. "Warren Buffett on Reputation: the Economic Value of Values, Integrity and Corporate Culture." available at https://finnpr.com/warren-buffett-reputation-berkshire-hathaway

Forbes. 2011. "Reverse Mentoring. What Is It and Why Is It Beneficial." available at https://forbes.com/sites/work-in-progress/2011/01/03/reverse-mentoring-what-is-it-and-why-is-it-beneficial/#6318e30e21cc

Forbes. 2012. "New Research Unlocks The Secret of Employee Recognition." available at https://forbes.com/sites/joshbersin/2012/06/13/new-research-unlocks-the-secret-of-employee-recognition/#5ec8337f5276

Forbes. 2013. "The Secret to Motivating Your Team." available at https://forbes.com/sites/dailymuse/2013/03/19/the-secret-to-motivating-your-team/#a1cd08f24d71

Forbes. 2013. "Your Company Vision: If It's Complicated, It Shouldn't Be." https://forbes.com/sites/johnkotter/2013/10/14/the-reason-most-company-vision-statements-arent-effective/#302f4d822dc7

Forbes. 2015. "10 New Findings About The Millennial Consumer." available at https://forbes.com/sites/danschawbel/2015/01/20/10-new-findings-about-the-millennial-consumer/#1e8fa6136c8f

Forbes. 2015. "90% of Startups Fail: Here's What You Need to Know About The 10%." available at https://forbes.com/sites/neilpatel/2015/01/16/90-of-startups-will-fail-heres-what-you-need-to-know-about-the-10/#33796d816679

Forbes. 2016. "Why Everyone Must Get Ready for 4th Industrial Revolution." available at https://forbes.com/sites/bernardmarr/2016/04/05/why-everyone-must-get-ready-for-4th-industrial-revolution/#60a6ab333f90

Forbes. 2018. "The Impact of AI on The HR Profession." available at https://forbes.com/sites/karenhigginbottom/2018/06/14/the-impact-of-ai-on-the-hr-profession/#5054876f91ca

Fortune. 2016. "How Fortune's "Change the World" Companies Profit From Doing Good." available at http://fortune.com/2016/08/18/change-world-companies-profit/

Fortune. 2017. "The 10 Biggest Business Scandals of 2017." available at http://fortune.com/2017/12/31/biggest-corporate-scandals-misconduct-2017-pr/

Fortune. 2017. "United Airlines CEO Oscar Munoz System Failure." available at http://fortune.com/2017/04/27/united-airlines-ceo-oscar-munoz-system-failure/

Fortune. 2018. "Fortune Global 500 List 2018." available at http://fortune.com/global500/list

Harvard Business Review. 2008. "Are You Using Recognition Effectively." available at https://hbr.org/2008/02/are-you-using-recognition-effe-1?autocomplete=true

Harvard Business Review. 2010. "How Will You Measure Your Life?." available at https://hbr.org/2010/07/how-will-you-measure-your-life

Harvard Business Review. 2012. "Mumbai's Models of Service Excellence." available at https://hbr.org/2012/11/mumbais-models-of-service-excellence

Harvard Business Review. 2016. "A Global Survey on The Ambiguous State of Employee Trust." available at https://hbr.org/2016/07/a-global-survey-on-the-ambiguous-state-of-employee-trust

Harvard Business Review. 2018. "Do Your Employees Feel Respected." available at https://hbr.org/2018/07/do-your-employees-feel-respected?autocomplete=true

Harvard Business Review. 2018. "VUCA." available at https://hbr.org/resources/images/article_assets/hbr/1401/F1401C_A_LG.gif

Harvard Business Review. 2018. "Why CEOs Devote So Much Time to Their Hobbies." available at https://hbr.org/2018/10/why-ceos-devote-so-much-time-to-their-hobbies?autocomplete=true

Harvard Business Review. July-August 2018. "Creating a Purpose-Driven Organization."

Hofstede, G., G.J. Hofstede, and M. Minkov. 2010. *Cultures and Organizations. Software of the Mind. Intercultural Cooperation and Its Importance for Survival.* McGraw Hill.

Huffington Post. 2017. "A Piece of Colored Ribbon." available at https://huffing tonpost.com/randy-pennington/a-piece-of-colored-ribbon_b_13440926. html

INC. 2005. "How I Did It: Reed Hastings, Netflix." available at https://inc.com/magazine/20051201/qa-hastings.html

INC. 2018. "Why Jeff Bezos Puts Relentless Focus on Amazon's Company Culture." available at https://inc.com/sonia-thompson/how-jeff-bezos-cultivates-a-culture-of-high-standards-at-amazon.html

Inc.com. 2017. "5 Industries A.I. Will Disrupt in The Next 10 Years." available at https://inc.com/james-paine/5-industries-ai-will-disrupt-in-the-next-10-years.html

Innosight, Strategy and Innovation at Huron. 2016. "Corporate Longevity: Turbulence Ahead for Large Organizations." available at https://innosight.com/wp-content/uploads/2016/08/Corporate-Longevity-2016-Final.pdf

Internet Live Stats. 2018. "Total Number of Websites." available at http://internetlivestats.com/total-number-of-websites/

Internet World Stats. 2018. "Internet Usage Statistics." Available at https://internetworldstats.com/stats.htm

Investopedia. 2011. "5 Successful Companies That Survived The Dotcom Bubble." available at https://investopedia.com/financial-edge/0711/5-successful-companies-that-survived-the-dotcom-bubble.aspx

Investopedia. 2015. "World's Top 10 Retailers." available at https://investopedia.com/articles/markets/122415/worlds-top-10-retailers-wmt-cost.asp

Jefferson, T., and W.P. Gardner. 1904–05. *The Works of Thomas Jefferson*, 11 Vols. Federal Edition. New York and London: G.P. Putnam's Sons.

John F. Kennedy Presidential Library and Museum. 2018. "Ask Not What Your Country Can Do For You." available at https://jfklibrary.org/Education/Teachers/Curricular-Resources/Elementary-School-Curricular-Materials/Ask-Not.aspx

Lake News Online. 2012. "30+ Year Walmart Employee Recalls Visits from Sam Walton." available at https://lakenewsonline.com/article/20120309/NEWS/303099838

Legge, K. 2002. "On Knowledge, Business Consultants, and the Selling of Total Quality Management." In *Critical Consulting*, eds. T. Clark and R. Fincham, 74–92. New York, NY: Wiley- Blackwell.

Life Hack. 2018. "Millennials and Their Spending Habits: How It's Shaping the World." available at https://lifehack.org/421652/millennials-and-their-spending-habits-how-its-shaping-the-world

Live Science. 2018. "How Big Is the Internet?" available at https://livescience.com/54094-how-big-is-the-internet.html

Mabey, C. 2011. *Leadership and HRM—UOL Study Guide.*

Marketing. 2018. "Marriott China in Crisis Comms Mode as Website Gets Shutdown." available at http://marketing-interactive.com/gallery-marriott-gaffe-now-snowballs-into-rule-setting-campaign/

Massachusetts Historical Society. 2018. "Digital Library: Letter from John Adams to Abigail Adams, post May 12, 1780." available at https://masshist.org/digitaladams/archive/popup?id=L17800512jasecond&page=L17800512jasecond_1

MerchDope. 2018. "YouTube Statistics." available at https://merchdope.com/youtube-statistics/

Mokyr, J. June 2017. "How Europe Won the Race to Prosperity." *BBC History Magazine* (*The History Essay*), pp. 41–46.

Monticello. 2018. "Thomas Jefferson and The Declaration of Independence." available at https://monticello.org/site/jefferson/jefferson-and-declaration

Monzo. 2018. "Monzo." available at https://monzo.com

Mount Holyoke. 2018. "India: Key Developments and Dates." available at https://mtholyoke.edu/courses/rschwart/hist151f08/India/key_developments&dates.htm

Navex Global. 2017. "Corporate America Has a Trust Problem. A Big One." available at https://navexglobal.com/blog/article/corporate-america-has-a-trust-problem-a-big-one/

Ogden, G. 1991. *The New Reformation: Returning the Ministry to the People of God.* Zondervan Publishing Company.

Parker, E. 1965. *Albert Camus, the Artist in the Arena.* University of Wisconsin Press.

Peace Corps. 2018. "Peace Corps." available at https://peacecorps.gov

Porter, M. 1985. *Competitive Advantage.* New York, NY: The Free Press.

Reuters. 2018. "Amazon Scraps Secret AI Recruiting Tool That Showed Bias Against Women." available at https://reuters.com/article/us-amazon-com-jobs-automation-insight/amazon-scraps-secret-ai-recruiting-tool-that-showed-bias-against-women-idUSKCN1MK08G

Richardson, L. 2011. "Sisyphus and Caesar: the Opposition of Greece and Rome in Albert Camus' Absurd Cycle." *Classical Receptions Journal* 4, no. 1, pp. 66–89.

Schein, E.H. 2004. *Organizational Culture and Leadership*, 3rd ed. San Francisco, CA: Jossey-Bass.

Schein, E.H. 2010. *Organizational Culture and Leadership*, Vol 2. Jossey-Bass.

Science Focus. 2018. "How Much Data is on The Internet." Available at http://sciencefocus.com/qa/how-many-terabytes-data-are-internet

South China Morning Post. 2018. Marriott Sacks Employee Who "like" Tibet Independence Group." available at http://scmp.com/news/china/society/article/2128124/marriott-sacks-employee-who-liked-twitter-post-tibet-independence#comments

Sustainable Brands. 2014. "BBVA, AT&T, GE, Unilever Among Brands Best at Making Sustainability Viral in 2013." available at https://sustainablebrands.com/news_and_views/marketing_comms/matthew_yeomans/bbva_att_ge_unilever_among_brands_best_making_sustain

Sustainable Brands. 2014. "Millennials Most Sustainability Conscious Generation Yet but Don't Call Them "Environmentalist"". available at https://sustainablebrands.com/news_and_views/stakeholder_trends_insights/aarthi_rayapura/millennials_most_sustainability_conscious

Tech Crunch. 2018. "Amazon Strikes $1 Trillion Market Cap, 4 Weeks After Apple Did The Same." available at https://techcrunch.com/2018/09/04/amazon-strikes-1-trillion-market-cap-4-weeks-after-apple-did-the-same/

The Daily Star. 2015. "Singapore at 50: From Third World to First." available at https://thedailystar.net/op-ed/politics/singapore-50-third-world-first-123337

The East India Company. 2018. "The East India Company Timeline." available at https://theeastindiacompany.com/the-east-india-company/timeline/

The Economist. 2018. "What's Really Driving Today's Young Innovators?" available at https://eiuperspectives.economist.com/strategy-leadership/entrepreneurs-perspective/infographic/whats-really-driving-todays-young-innovators?utm_source=Paid%20Social&utm_medium=LinkedIn_ROW_young%20Innovators&utm_campaign=FedEx%20-%20An%20entrepreneur%27s%20perspective&utm_content=Infographic

The Free Dictionary by FARLEX. 2018. "New Economy" available at https://encyclopedia2.thefreedictionary.com/New+Economy

The New York Times. 2016. "Presidential Election Results: Donald J. Trump Wins." available at https://nytimes.com/elections/results/president

The Next Web. 2018. "Amazon Pulls Work Culture Out of The Shitter Ahead of HQ2 Opening." available at https://thenextweb.com/insights/2018/06/22/report-amazon-pulls-work-culture-out-of-the-shitter-ahead-of-hq2-opening/

The Nobel Prize. 2018. "Christian Lange." available at http://nobelprize.org/nobel_prizes/peace/laureates/1921/lange-bio.html

The Richest. 2012. "Craig Silverstein." available at https://therichest.com/celebnetworth/celebrity-business/men/craig-silverstein-net-worth/

The Telegraph. 2013. "Why Learn A Foreign Language? Benefits of Bilingualism." https://telegraph.co.uk/education/educationopinion/10126883/Why-learn-a-foreign-language-Benefits-of-bilingualism.html

The Very Well Mind. 2018. "The Five Levels of Maslow's Hierarchy of Needs." available at https://verywellmind.com/what-is-maslows-hierarchy-of-needs-4136760

The Victorian Web. 2013. "The British East India Company- the Company That Owned a Nation (or Two)." available at http://victorianweb.org/history/empire/india/eic.html

The Washington Post. 2018. "China Asked Marriott to Shut Down Its Website. The Company Complied." available at https://washingtonpost.com/news/business/wp/2018/01/18/china-demanded-marriott-change-its-website-the-company-complied/?noredirect=on&utm_term=.00ee1a063845

The World Bank. 2017. "Powered by Education, East Asia Is Getting Ready For the Fourth Industrial Revolution." available at http://blogs.worldbank.org/education/insidetheweb/education-east-asia-fourth-industrial-revolution

Time Magazine. 2016. "The Making of President Donald Trump." available at http://time.com/4564440/donald-trump-wins-2/

Totally Timelines. 2018. "East India Company 1600-1873." available at https://totallytimelines.com/east-india-company-1600-1873/

U.S. Securities and Exchange Commission. 1998. "Amazon CEO Jeff Bezo's Letter to Share Holders." available at https://sec.gov/Archives/edgar/data/1018724/000119312518121161/d456916dex991.htm

United Continental Holdings. 2018. "Company Information." available at http://ir.united.com/company-information/company-overview

Veiga, J.F., and J. Pfeffer. 1999. "Putting People First for Organizational Success." *The Academy of Management Executive* (1993–2005) 13, no. 2, pp. 37–48.

Walton, S. 1993. *Sam Walton. Made in America.* New York, NY: Bantam Books.

Wargamer. 2015. "The Battle of Waterloo and Napoleon's Immortals–The Old Guard." https://wargamer.com/articles/the-battle-of-waterloo-and-napoleons-immortals-the-old-guard/

WBUR. 2017. "Facebook CEO Mark Zuckerberg, A Harvard Dropout , Delivers Commencement Speech." available at http://wbur.org/news/2017/05/25/zuckerberg-harvard-commencement

Wikiepdia. 2018. "History of YouTube." available at https://en.wikipedia.org/wiki/History_of_YouTube

Wikipedia. 2017. "Otto Kahn-Freund." available at https://en.wikipedia.org/wiki/Otto_Kahn-Freund

Wikipedia. 2018. " History of Nokia." available at https://en.wikipedia.org/wiki/History_of_Nokia

Wikipedia. 2018. "Alan Turing." available at https://en.wikipedia.org/wiki/Alan_Turing

Wikipedia. 2018. "Albert Camus." available at https://en.wikipedia.org/wiki/Albert_Camus#cite_note-3

Wikipedia. 2018. "Bantam Presidency." available at https://en.wikipedia.org/wiki/Bantam_Presidency

Wikipedia. 2018. "Battle of Lodi." available at https://en.wikipedia.org/wiki/Battle_of_Lodi

Wikipedia. 2018. "Bill Clinton." available at https://en.wikipedia.org/wiki/Bill_Clinton

Wikipedia. 2018. "Christian Lous Lange." available at https://en.wikipedia.org/wiki/Christian_Lous_Lange

Wikipedia. 2018. "Doug McMillon: Revision History." available at https://en.wikipedia.org/wiki/Doug_McMillon

Wikipedia. 2018. "Forbes Global 2000." available at https://en.wikipedia.org/wiki/Forbes_Global_2000

Wikipedia. 2018. "James Lancaster." available at https://en.wikipedia.org/wiki/James_Lancaster

Wikipedia. 2018. "Jean Lannes." available at https://en.wikipedia.org/wiki/Jean_Lannes

Wikipedia. 2018. "John Watts." available at https://en.wikipedia.org/wiki/John_Watts_(merchant)#cite_note-Bicheno-1

Wikipedia. 2018. "Siege of Toulon." available at https://en.wikipedia.org/wiki/Siege_of_Toulon

Wikipedia. 2018. "The Battle of Waterloo." available at https://en.wikipedia.org/wiki/Battle_of_Waterloo#cite_note-FOOTNOTELongford1971547-43

Wikipedia. 2018. "The Empire on Which The Sun Never Sets." available at https://en.wikipedia.org/wiki/The_empire_on_which_the_sun_never_sets

Wikipedia. 2018. "The Four Great Inventions." available at https://en.wikipedia.org/wiki/Four_Great_Inventions

Wikipedia. 2018. "United Airlines." available at https://en.wikipedia.org/wiki/United_Airlines

Wikipedia. 2018. "Victorian Era." available at https://en.wikipedia.org/wiki/Victorian_era

Wikipedia. 2018. "Walmart." available at https://en.wikipedia.org/wiki/Walmart

Wikipedia. 2018. "Watt's West Indies and Virginia Expedition." available at https://en.wikipedia.org/wiki/Watts%27_West_Indies_and_Virginia_expedition

Wikipedia. 2018. "John Adams." available at https://en.wikipedia.org/wiki/John_Adams#cite_note-72

Wired. 2016. "Hey, Nokia Isn't Just a Company That Used to Make Phones." available at https://wired.com/2016/04/hey-nokia-isnt-just-company-used-make-phones/

World Economic Forum. 2018. "Five Facts You Need to Understand the New Global Order." available at https://weforum.org/agenda/2018/01/five-facts-you-need-to-understand-the-new-global-order/

York University. 2000. "A Theory of Human Motivation by A.H. Maslow (1943)." available at http://psychclassics.yorku.ca/Maslow/motivation.htm

About the Authors

Ivan Yong Wei Kit is an Organizational Psychologist, engineer, entrepreneur and a startup angel investor based in Hong Kong. In his capacity as an organizational psychologist, he was instrumental in strategizing and executing Fortune 500 and startup human capital strategy in a diverse cultural setting of Asia Pacific. He believes in not just having the "right talent" but also the "right culture" to bring about exponential organizational performances. He had also worked with the Malaysian government in helping state funded startups to build a successful team through cultural formation, psychometric assessment and coaching. He co-founded Nanyang Angelz, an angel's network of Nanyang Technological University (NTU), Singapore Alumnus in China, Hong Kong and ASEAN. Nanyang Angelz seeks to add value as an early stage investor through providing market access via its network. He is also the founding member of the European Mentoring and Coaching Council, Asia Pacific Chapter as a Vice President of Solidarity.

He holds a Bachelor of Engineering (Mechanical and Production) with Honors from NTU, Singapore, a MSc. in Organizational Psychology from the University of London and a Diploma in Child Psychology from the Open University of Hong Kong. Wei Kit is a keen language learner and is fluent in English, Malay, Mandarin, Cantonese and Japanese.

Sam Lee is a career Human Resources professional and an entrepreneur since 1997. He is very much involved in the startup scene and has co-founded Nanyang Angelz, a network of marketplace professionals/ private investors, to provide angel funding for startups and marketplace advisory services. GENUS is a social venture he co-founded, and this startup supports underprivileged children in Asia to learn English.

Sam is also active in the human resources industries. He co-founded Banking Talents in Shanghai and Corban Group International in Hong Kong, providing executive searches for MNCs and SMEs alike. His work covers China, Hong Kong, and regional countries.

Sam holds a Bachelor Degree in Engineering from NTU, Singapore. His other professional qualifications are Graduate Diploma in Marketing Management, Diploma in Human Resources Development from Singapore Institute of Management in Singapore, and is a Certified PDA Analyst (for Personality Profiling). Sam is a member of the Hong Kong Society of Economists, where he also edits and publishes the "Hong Kong Society of Economists Magazine." He is also a member of the Departmental Advisory Committee of the Department of Linguistic and Translation, City University of Hong Kong.

Index

OTHER TITLES IN THE ENTREPRENEURSHIP AND SMALL BUSINESS MANAGEMENT COLLECTION

Scott Shane, Case Western University, Editor

- *African American Entrepreneurs: Successes and Struggles of Entrepreneurs of Color in America* by Michelle Ingram Spain and J. Mark Munoz
- *How to Get Inside Someone's Mind and Stay There: The Small Business Owner's Guide to Content Marketing and Effective Message Creation* by Jacky Fitt
- *Profit: Plan for It, Get It—The Entrepreneurs Handbook* by H.R Hutter
- *Understanding the Family Business: Exploring the Differences Between Family and Nonfamily Businesses, Second Edition* by Keanon J. Alderson
- *Navigating Entrepreneurship: 11 Proven Keys to Success* by Larry Jacobson
- *Global Women in the Start-up World: Conversations in Silicon Valley* by Marta Zucker
- *Getting to Market With Your MVP: How to Achieve Small Business and Entrepreneur Success* by J.C. Baker

Announcing the Business Expert Press Digital Library

Concise e-books business students need for classroom and research

This book can also be purchased in an e-book collection by your library as

- a one-time purchase,
- that is owned forever,
- allows for simultaneous readers,
- has no restrictions on printing, and
- can be downloaded as PDFs from within the library community.

Our digital library collections are a great solution to beat the rising cost of textbooks. E-books can be loaded into their course management systems or onto students' e-book readers.
The **Business Expert Press** digital libraries are very affordable, with no obligation to buy in future years. For more information, please visit **www.businessexpertpress.com/librarians**. To set up a trial in the United States, please email **sales@businessexpertpress.com**.

www.ingramcontent.com/pod-product-compliance
Lightning Source LLC
Chambersburg PA
CBHW061336220326
41599CB00026B/5207